10-23-50

D1061926

DATE DUE

About the Book

Private enterprise is fighting for its life, and many people do not realize it. It is in a deadly conflict with the ideology of collectivism and controlled economy. Freedom must be the first concern of every American.

The greatest peril facing America in the post-war world is here carefully discussed. The Biblical basis of our private enterprise system and the validity of the profit motive are presented. Freedom for America will be in even greater danger, following the war. The leftist and radical movements in the United States, as they are being led and provided with wisdom by the carefully planned propaganda of the Federal Council of the Churches of Christ in America, are here thoroughly unmasked and exposed.

Mr. McIntire points out that the assault upon private enterprise is devious, and that America is being unsuspectedly given the ideology of totalitarianism in the terms of the Christian Church. In fact, the so-called kingdom of God, as being presented to America at the present moment under the dominant leadership of the Protestant forces, is nothing more than the collectivism of Karl Marx, and it involves the tyranny of Russia.

The different uses of the words "democracy," "liberty," and the like are carefully presented, and the confusion involved in their general use today is pointed out.

The only remedy for this condition is offered. In order to preserve our liberty, we must return to the Bible which gave it to us. The view of the individual as presented in Scripture, in the creeds of the Church, and in the Constitution of the United States is the heritage of every free American. The present-day modern church, under the leadership of the Federal Council, has departed from these.

The book is stirring. It is breath-taking in its revelations and should be read by every American.

The issues in the battle with the Russian ideology are the issues of this volume. The cost of appeasement and compromise is vividly portrayed. America must continue the battle for freedom.

About the Author

The Rev. Carl McIntire is pastor of the Bible Presbyterian Church, Collingswood, N. J., a congregation which has a membership of more than 1500. Fifty cents out of every dollar received in the church goes for benevolences. The total giving of the congregation for all of its work during its fiscal year of 1944-1945 was more than $110,000.

Mr. McIntire is the president of the Board of Directors of Faith Theological Seminary, Wilmington, Del., a member of the Independent Board for Presbyterian Foreign Missions, a member of the Board of Directors of the National Bible Institute, New York, and of the Harvey Cedars Bible Presbyterian Conference, Harvey Cedars, N. J.

In 1936 he started the *Christian Beacon*, a weekly religious newspaper and, ever since, has been its publisher and editor. The *Christian Beacon* has an international circulation and vigorously defends the historic Christian faith as opposed to the collectivism that is discussed in this volume.

In 1941 Mr. McIntire had a part in the establishment of the American Council of Christian Churches and served as its first president.

He was born May 17, 1906.

THE RISE

of

THE TYRANT

Controlled Economy vs. Private Enterprise

By

CARL McINTIRE

Pastor of the Bible Presbyterian Church
Collingswood, N. J.

1945

CHRISTIAN BEACON PRESS

Collingswood, New Jersey

Drawing for jacket by Harry W. Veatch

PREFACE

AMERICA faces the greatest struggle of her existence. In the postwar world the conflict between a free economy and the Russian idea of controlled economy will produce its severest conflict within the United States. We endeavor here to point out that the basic difference between the two is religious and that America is being led to embrace the ideas that inevitably produce tyranny.

The leadership for this struggle against free enterprise is being furnished by the most respectable sources. Here is given a description of the forces organizing to destroy our way of freedom, and the equipment every Christian man who loves America must have in order to preserve it.

The substance of this book was first presented in a series of radio messages on Sunday evenings from the pulpit of the Bible Presbyterian Church in Collingswood, which messages were entitled, "Private Enterprise in the Scriptures." The public response and the encouragement of the officials of the church have led to the reorganizing of the material and its presentation in this form.

During it all we have had the encouragement and the constant prayers of our people, for which we are most thankful. The work could not have been done without the untiring efforts of Miss Ethel Rink, secretary of the church; Miss Helen M. Lord, proofreader of *The Sunday School Times;* and Mrs. Ruth P. Grubb, teacher in the Collingswood High School. Others, too, have helped. There has been a feeling on the part of all that it is the cause of the Lord Jesus Christ, and in that spirit it has been a genuine labor of love.

vii

Every effort has been made to be fair, accurate, and careful, even to an understating of the case, so that the greatest possible good may be accomplished.

We thank the various publishing companies for granting us permission to quote from their works. The titles are listed in the back of the book.

Collingswood, New Jersey   CARL McINTIRE.
May, 1945

CONTENTS

INTRODUCTION

WHEN freedom is destroyed, whatever takes its place is tyranny. There is no substitute for freedom. Only in a free society can man be man. Private enterprise, which we cherish for America, can live only in a free economy. Destroy liberty and you kill private enterprise. Limit private enterprise and you massacre freedom. What is separately spoken of today as "political freedom" and "economic freedom" are one and the same, and to attempt to separate them is to open the door for the tyrant.

The problems that face us in America today—the enjoyment of our democracy, the maintenance of private enterprise, the preservation of a free economy, and the security of our liberties—are, at bottom, religious issues. These realities came out of the abiding faith of our forefathers who believed certain things about God, about man, about the Bible. Because they believed these things they gave us the land in which we dwell, a land of liberty.

This is primarily a religious book. The whole question of private enterprise is here examined from the viewpoint of religion and the Scriptures. It is, definitely, not a political treatise. It does not go into politics. It is written on the assumption that partisan politics and religion are two different spheres of activity; and a minister, if he wishes to preach and to be an effective servant, should stay out of such politics. There are, however, deep, abiding principles inherent in religious teaching and dogma—and we use the word "dogma" deliberately—which should be presented by the church, and which form the solid foundation stones upon which our free society stands. With these issues the preacher must deal!

This book is not a treatise on economics. Some preachers today have decided that it is their calling to become specialists in the field of economics. The reason for this is that they have abandoned the historical concept of the prophet. We do not share this view. However, the foundation stones of the economic world have a direct relationship to the structure of the world itself as God created it.

This book makes an appeal to authority, an authority beyond the powers of this world, an authority which many today no longer desire to respect or credit. We credit it; we believe it. The men who made America what it is believed it; they were so obedient to its message that they wrote upon our coins, "In God we trust." The authority to which we appeal is none other than the Bible, the Book that our fathers and mothers read and loved and explained to us when we were little ones about the home.

Though we make no claim to present the matter on the basis of politics or economics, we do make a claim to present the matter in the light of God's Word. We have given our life as a specialist in the Scriptures, finding their exact meaning in the Greek and Hebrew, and defending their doctrines which not only have given us the moral structure of our civilization but also have presented to the world the Church of Jesus Christ and the message of eternal life.

Since God, who gave us the Bible, is also the God of creation, His Word and creation agree. The so-called economic laws which we find written in nature, immutable, agree with the eternal moral laws written in the Scriptures.

We want this approach to the subject of private enterprise to be fresh and different; we hope that it will inject into the current public debate at the present moment an entirely new field for the consideration of men. It may be called a new field because it has been so completely ignored in recent years. The truth for the support of private enterprise and the capitalistic system that we here present is the basis that originally gave it its existence; it is the basis that alone gives lasting conviction, a passion that persists, and a faith that will enable men to suffer, sacrifice, and die for the maintenance of private enterprise, a free economy, and the liberties that are inherent therein.

We have a general thesis. This thesis is that the Bible teaches private enterprise and the capitalistic system, not as a by-product or as some side line, but as the very foundation structure of society itself in which men are to live and render an account of themselves to God.

This thesis must be expounded and defended because it is under attack. Strangely, it is under attack today by the very men and groups who should be presenting to us the thesis itself. These include high leaders in many Protestant churches, some of our larger Protestant denominations, as expressed through their official pronouncements; and, more emphatically, by the one body that claims to represent the Protestant churches in their joint capacity, the Federal Council of the Churches of Christ in America.

Here is an illustration of what we mean. January 15-19, 1945, under the direction of the Federal Council of the Churches of Christ in America, a second national study conference on the subject of "A Just and Durable Peace" was held at Cleveland, Ohio. In dealing with the subject of peace it adopted certain letters to the churches. Mr. Russell Porter, writing in the New York *Times* of this meeting, stated that the message "said that changes in the American economic system might be necessary in the direction of more social planning and control with more regulation of the rights of private property and freedom of enterprise."

One of the delegates to this conference was the editor of the Muskegon *Chronicle,* Muskegon, Michigan. The meeting opened his eyes and alarmed him beyond measure. He went back to Muskegon and wrote a searching editorial showing his alarm at the Federal Council's departure from the principles of private enterprise and individual responsibility. He said, "A declaration for out-and-out socialization of the economic system of America would have been infinitely more popular with that group.

"To the professional leadership of organized religion in America, take it by and large with notable exceptions, has been 'sold' the socialistic fallacy with magnificent thoroughness. There is a sort of holy enthusiasm for the cause.

"With it goes abysmal lack of comprehension of what is happening to America, blindness to the principle enunciated in the amendment thus summarily disposed of, that when government has assumed complete control of the economic life of a nation, as it is doing at an accelerated pace here, control of government—human freedom—will have been exchanged for control of the people by government—tyranny.

"And we churchmen have been too busy with our own affairs to intervene when that philosophy is proclaimed to be the voice of the church."

Yes, it is long past time to sound the alarm! Surely, a Christian minister who sees these issues clearly—as this editor from Muskegon has enunciated them here—should take it upon himself to analyze, to correlate, and then to narrate, in as simple a way as possible for the benefit and blessing of the average layman, the whole attack upon private enterprise as it is made by "the voice of the church."

It is to this task that we now turn. We give our heart and mind to it with a firm conviction that in the maintenance of the system of private enterprise the very life and liberty of the church itself are involved. Destroy a society based on private enterprise, and whatever system replaces it will be controlled. It involves tyranny, and the Christian church itself will go down, bound in the iron chains.

Part I

THE WORD OF GOD

CHAPTER 1

THE PRE-EMINENCE OF LIBERTY

"LIBERTY" and "freedom" are perhaps the most frequently used and best loved words in America today. We have inherited a free society. We have been fighting for freedom. The blood of the very finest of the young men of our nation has been poured out on the battlefields of the world to preserve freedom. One bit of evidence of the present love of freedom is the song hit, "Don't Fence Me In," which has been listed as one of the most popular in America.

We have no need to fear for our freedom from external enemies; at least, not for the present. We are too strong. The one place we need to be on our guard is on the inside. It has been said that we may win the war for freedom on the battlefield and lose the war for freedom on the home front. We take our liberties for granted; we assume that our democracy is secure; we believe our way of life is permanent. It is in such an attitude that peril lies. On the other hand, now that we have been fighting and sacrificing to maintain these liberties, any attack upon them internally, if it were, in any way, an open or a professed attack, would meet immediate resistance; and by our democratic processes we would keep it from coming to power politically.

It has been because of our freedom—our free economy, our free enterprise, our free system of education, our free medicine, our freedom of religion—that we have been able, as a nation, to rally to the defense of these ideals, and to come forth from the battlefields victorious.

Consequently, any attack upon our liberty would have

to be in such a subtle and unrecognizable form that the people would be unaware of its nature and unable to detect it until it had advanced to such a stage that irreparable harm had been done.

It is the purpose of this book to point out that such an attack—of the most serious nature and of the most far-reaching consequences—is being made today. It is coming from the most unexpected quarter, and it is making unbelievable advances. This attack, of course, is being made in the name of freedom. Freedom and liberty, the idols of the hour, cannot be replaced unless we are offered in their stead other idols that go by the same name. The popular slogans of this attack are on the lips of people everywhere. It is "economic democracy" as well as political democracy that we are told we must have. There must be a planned society instead of the chaos that lack of control permits. The profit motive with its "barbarous instinct" must be replaced by a higher and more lofty motive of service to one's fellow men. The rugged individualism of the past has had its day, and we must move on now into the security and comfort of a "democratically" controlled economy. The rights of property must be re-examined. The whole basis of society must be changed from one of competition to one of co-operation. Instead of the feud of competition we must have the co-operation of brotherhood. So runs the general nature of the attack.

These and similar slogans are being held up before us today in every possible manner. As a nation and as a people we are urged to press on to attain them. When, however, we are told that the basis of society must be changed from one of competition, one in which the profit motive is at work, to some other foundation, we have set before us the real seriousness of what is actually happening. Society has a basis. It has a foundation. When you change that basis, you shake society itself. As a matter of fact, you tear down the house. It is one thing to jack up a house and remove a crumbling foundation in order to replace it with another foundation that will support the same house; but it is another thing to tear out the foundation of a house and then rebuild the foundation to support a superstructure of an entirely different plan and nature.

When we talk about the social control of economic processes for the common good, we have an entirely different kind of foundation upon which to build society from the society in which we have had free enterprise where the elements of the profit motive, competition, and individualism have had full sway. To change the basis of society in such a way is revolutionary. Society has been operating on its present basis for many centuries. To turn it all over and start out anew, or, more realistically, to attempt to change the foundation and to remodel the superstructure while the family lived in the house would be more than exasperating to the housewife, and much more so to the bewildered children and distracted husband.

This is the nature of the attack, and in it are involved the very liberties for which we have fought. We have held before us four freedoms. The first two of these freedoms, as they are popularly considered, are logically contradictory and incompatible with the last two, and yet very few people realize this. We shall discuss them more in detail later on.

We expect attack upon the American way of life from the radical elements, from the communistic elements, but we certainly do not expect good Americans, men who love freedom, to be a party to an ideology of any kind that will undermine our precious freedoms. The point is that when people are a party to such propaganda they are unwittingly promoting the cause that later they will regret with tears.

The ideas that are expressed in the foregoing popular slogans are a part of an ideology. It is this ideology that the modern church, in a holy crusade, is now preaching and holding up before the Christians of America as the goal of liberty toward which we must now move. The attacks that have been made upon private enterprise in the last twenty-five years have had little opposition from the church. In fact the church has aided in the attacks. Of course there are abuses connected with private enterprise and the capitalistic system, and no one could possibly condemn them and cry for their reproof more than we do, but these can and will be singled out. The attack of the modern church has not been upon these evils alone; it has been upon the very heart and core of the existence of private enterprise. It is the "sinful" profit motive and "wicked" competitive order that must be changed! This is the spearhead of the attack.

It is these increasingly popular ideas, which the church is now offering to the nation and the people, that are wrong —wrong in the sense that they are contrary to the historic position of the church; yea, even more than that, they are contrary to the eternal truth of God as revealed in His Scriptures and as made known to us in creation and providence.

The last place in the world from which you would expect an attack of any kind upon liberty or upon those things that are essential to liberty would be the church. The church should be the guardian of liberty. Because people believe that the church should be the guardian and defender of liberty, they are ready to listen to the message of the church and to accept it as the road to freedom and the more abundant life. Because of the confidence people have in the church in its place in society, the place that society has given it by virtue of its historic position and place of blessing and power, here is the most advantageous place imaginable for the presentation of erroneous ideas. In other words, when people listen to the church, they are disarmed. When the profit motive is attacked by the preacher, private enterprise reels and staggers under the blows. Yet people will listen, believing that they should hear about their sin—the sin of the profit motive.

In laying the groundwork for the structure of this thesis, the seriousness of it all can be seen by the size and magnitude of the church, which is making this attack. This attack upon private enterprise and the profit motive is made not by some isolated churches here and there. No, it is made in the name of the Federal Council of the Churches of Christ in America. The Federal Council claims to represent twenty-five million people. It represents twenty-five denominations and 150,000 Protestant churches in the United States. (The number of denominations mentioned here has been reduced to twenty-four, upon the action of the Reformed Episcopal Church, on May 24, 1945, withdrawing from the Federal Council. This will alter the Federal Council's own claim quoted throughout this book.) The attack is made in the name of this multitude. It is the voice of this Council that is telling us that the basis of society must be changed, and that the social control of the economic processes for the common good should be brought to pass.

Time for February 6th, reporting the Cleveland conference to which we referred in our introduction, where 450 leaders of the Protestant churches, under the auspices of the Federal Council, met to discuss the basis of "A Just and Durable Peace," announced that the late President Roosevelt, in receiving the unqualified endorsement of that body for the Dumbarton Oaks Proposals, had received the support of the most substantial body of public opinion in the United States. Yet this was the group which, in addition to the consideration of the Dumbarton Oaks Proposals, announced that the whole basis of property, as it has always been understood in the history of this country, needs to be revised. Later we shall give this evidence and discuss the matter in detail. We mention it here to show the magnitude and the far-reaching nature of the attack. The ideology underlying our system of freedom is being assaulted by another ideology which involves the philosophy of collectivism.

Now, at the outset of this discussion, as we begin to tell this story, we want it to be clearly understood that we are in no way exposing or attacking individuals as such. We are confident that if these men fully realized what they are doing they would stop. Our only explanation of their attitude, as we shall continue, is that they do not understand, that they have been blinded. We are not against the church. God forbid such a thought! We are for the church, as this story will evidence. It is because of our deep love for the historic church of Christ and its place of power and blessing to civilization that we have heeded the call, assumed the burden of this volume, and are now undertaking to mark the road on which the tyrant will ride. As the pastor of a church, the last thing in the world we should want to see would be that the church of Christ should suffer; but it must *be* the church of Christ, the church that is standing upon the rock of His eternal Word and defending the heritage that is ours in the written record. To the church has come the clarion call of "Thus saith the Lord," the certainty, the authority of a message from Heaven. But when the church of Christ turns aside from the Word, aside from a belief in its finality, inerrancy, and authority, then it gets into real trouble.

The deceptiveness and the tragedy of the present emphasis of the church, as represented through the Federal Council and its leaders as they push their crusade in the name of "economic democracy," is that they have identified it with the kingdom of God. It is to them the fullness of the Gospel, and they advocate it with a holy passion, making it the theme song of gatherings and the constant topic of book after book. As the impact of this comes upon our American people, they think it is the cause of Christ. In the name of the living God, slogans and ideas, which when they come to fruition will mean a revolution in the nature and basis of our social order, are being pressed upon the public, and especially given to the minds of the younger generation. The church is preaching these things in this way because it does not want violence to bring in the change, or "the kingdom." It wants to make this program of a planned economy the common faith of all men in such a way that it can be put into effect by the democratic, political processes without violence or bloodshed, so that there will be very little protest or possibility for objection to the matter when it actually comes to pass.

Dr. G. Bromley Oxnam, Methodist bishop of the New York area and president of the Federal Council, in his recent volume, published late in 1944, "Preaching in a Revolutionary Age," has this to say, on the first page:

"Revolution is a period of action in which faith must become works. A common faith must become a common purpose resulting in a common act. If there can be general agreement upon the question of ends, violence may be avoided when considering the question of means. Failure to unite in a common faith means conflict, because respect for law passes when large sections of the community no longer believe the law to be expressive of the common desire."

Can it be possible that, while we are fighting a war for liberty, the church of Jesus Christ within our own gates is preaching to us ideas that will take from us the very liberty for which our boys have died? This is the prospect that alarms us, the situation, as substantiated by irrefutable facts, we believe now to exist. If we can prove our case, we shall have rendered to the cause of Christ a service of invaluable proportions. The evidence is so abundant, once it is pointed out, that the task is not difficult.

The true church defends the profit motive, competition, private enterprise, and the individual, on the authority of the Word of God. The modern church, on the other hand, under the leadership of the Federal Council, attacks these. Both groups preach to the whole country. Both groups talk about the kingdom of God. Both groups mean entirely different things by their terms. Yet they talk with the same phrases, use the same Biblical words, and promote their causes with the same apparent earnestness.

It reminds us of an illustration. During the battle of the Belgian Bulge, one reason the Germans were able to make such tremendous advances was that, riding in American jeeps and dressed in American uniforms, came German soldiers who could speak good English. In outward appearance they looked exactly like a good American outfit, but the direction in which they drove and the ideas that motivated the drivers determined the side and the loyalty of the group. Of course, it was confusing; but when the Americans realized that such jeeps were running around, they were on the alert, and they soon were able to overcome this subtlety.

Now that we have made charges, there must be some

basis by which we can judge as to who is right. Is the present basis of our society really wrong? Should we move on to an economically controlled and planned society? In answering these questions, and also in holding up the position of the Federal Council as being erroneous, it is first incumbent upon us to establish the truth—the eternal truth —concerning the individual, concerning private enterprise, concerning the profit motive, concerning competition, concerning all these essential ingredients of a free economy as it has been revealed to us by God in His Word. If we can establish the reality of these things upon the authority of God's Word, then we have a standard of judgment, in the light of which we can perfectly evaluate the present crusade for a controlled economy.

CHAPTER 2

PRIVATE ENTERPRISE IN THE SCRIPTURES

THERE are two reasons why we are making this appeal to the Scriptures. First, we want the ideas of Scripture. What does the Bible teach about the individual and private enterprise? The teaching of the Bible is not manifold; it is one. What is the ideology of the Scriptures in regard to the social order? We want this information not just for the purpose of evaluating the error in the teaching of the Federal Council of the Churches of Christ in America; we want this information because of its own inherent value. The Bible's idea is true, and any departures from it into various fields of collectivism will take different forms. It makes no difference whether it is communism, national socialism, or national fascism, it is all tyranny. The departure into these fields, so far as human thought is concerned, always takes place at the point where the false idea enters. Since the Federal Council, for instance, is so interested in propagating, in every possible way, its idea for the changing of our social order, we think it is time—yea, it is long past time—for the teaching of the Scriptures to be brought out again into the light where men can see it, propagate it, and use it as a basis for their position and argument against any and every form and shade of collectivism.

Moreover, the second reason for this appeal is that it represents the position of God. Ideas, of course, commend themselves to men because they personally believe they are true, but the human mind is sinful and perverted; sometimes it rests in positions that are, in themselves, false because the human mind is colored and clouded by sin. Therefore, we need to have set before us in all of its clarity, without spot or blemish, the eternal truth of God. The Creator made the universe; He has established it and the foundations thereof. I am one who believes that the Bible is His special revelation. He has spoken to us in it once and for all time. In this deposit of truth everything that we need for life and happiness He has given. We are neither to add to it nor to take from it, but in simple faith to receive it, believe it, and seek to carry out its commandments. I bow before the supreme authority of God's Word. It is above fallible and human reason, and yet it is not contrary to true thought, for it is the truth. God, who knows everything, has given us this order for our life and living together.

The teaching of the Bible on this subject can be set forth under several different heads. In order to present the teaching clearly, so far as this discussion is concerned, let us say, first, that private enterprise is presupposed and established in the moral law; that is, in the Ten Commandments. This is the only moral law that exists, and anything that is called the moral law outside of the Ten Commandments is a misnomer. It is the particular command, "Thou shalt not steal," that deals with private enterprise. Here the right of property is established upon the authority of God. This right is permanent. This right is as eternal as God's law. A man has a right to hold property. No one can take this property from him. It is his. It is his by virtue of God's apportionment. He may use it; he may give it away; he may hide it. It is his to do with as he pleases. This, as we shall see later, is what the modern church calls selfishness. There is not the slightest thought here of the community of property, such as is suggested in collectivism, the social ownership and control of the economic processes. This command is a part of the whole decalogue; it finds its place in the entirety of God's command to the individual.

The First Commandment tells the individual that he must have no other gods but the true God. The Second Commandment tells the individual how he is to worship that God—not with graven images, but in spirit and in truth. The Third Commandment tells the individual that he shall not take the name of God in vain. His life and conduct, in relation to God, should be of a certain nature. The Fourth Commandment tells the individual that he must keep one day in seven for rest and worship of God. The Fifth Commandment establishes the home, the family, as the unit of society, and provides for the early care and training of the individual, not by the State, but by the parents. The Sixth Commandment guarantees the individual the right to live. We have no right to take another man's life. The Seventh Commandment demands the individual's purity. The purity of society is built upon each individual's purity. The Eighth Commandment guarantees the individual's right of property. Life, purity, property are individual, personal things. Property must be obtained in a lawful manner. We cannot steal another man's money.

The securing of property by the individual, however, in lawful ways, is private enterprise! The enterprising individual goes forth to secure and add to his property, for it is by his property that he eats, sleeps, and covers his head with a house. As he goes forth, he finds that all the other individuals have gone forth also; he discovers himself in a world where he is competing with other men. One cannot protect or add to private property without competition. It is just as immoral to take away a man's property and put him in a communal state, where everybody owns everything, as it would be to take away men's wives and let everybody

own all the wives! To do the former will also contribute
to the latter.

When our Federal Council friends talk about the planned
social order and economic democracy and attack individualism, we turn in reply and say, "Read the Ten Commandments. They form the most individualistic document that
the world has ever seen. They are the eternal bill of rights
of the individual." It is no wonder that those who feel the
force of individualism in the Ten Commandments want to
tone them down or discredit them by attacking them as
being "negative."

It has been in the honoring and the maintenance of these
Commandments that we have had our "God-planned" free
society. I have just used the word "planned." It is God's
order, God's plan, and, in carrying out this order, our social
laws have protected private property and the right of the
individual to the fruits of his own labor. We have set up
our statutes against immorality, and we have enacted our
laws against murder. Consequently, any organization or
group that would attack the right of private property is
attacking the eternal truth of God; he is chopping away at
the structure that holds up the individual. God's law is
eternal; that means that no matter what may be the development or the progress of society through the years, these
conditions and these moral standards must be maintained.

A man who has property, however, is a capitalist. He uses
his property for gain, and this capitalistic system of free
economy is recognized throughout the entire Bible. Abraham was a capitalist. Abraham and Lot tried to have a
community affair for a while, but they found it did not work,
so they divided their goods, separated, and each one went
his way, free. Isaac and Jacob were capitalists, but Jacob
paid a terrific price for his crookedness. It never really pays

in a capitalistic economy to be crooked! It does pay in a controlled economy to be crooked! Witness the profitable black market of the days of the O.P.A.

Moses was a real capitalist. When Moses was threatening Pharaoh in Egypt, crying, "Let my people go," one of the temptations that Moses refused was the offer of Pharaoh to let the Children of Israel depart from Egypt if they would only leave their property. Moses replied that they would not go if they could not take their property—their oxen and sheep. Moses told the Children of Israel: "If a man shall steal an ox, or a sheep, and kill it, or sell it; he shall restore five oxen for an ox, and four sheep for a sheep. . . . If a man shall deliver unto his neighbour money or stuff to keep, and it be stolen out of the man's house; if the thief be found, let him pay double" (Exod. 22:1, 7).

There is one element in this picture of private enterprise and private responsibility that the social planners have completely forgotten. The Prophet Hosea emphasizes it for us in a stern and withering passage: "Hear the word of the Lord, ye children of Israel: for the Lord hath a controversy with the inhabitants of the land, because there is no truth, nor mercy, nor knowledge of God in the land. By swearing, and lying, and killing, and stealing, and committing adultery, they break out, and blood toucheth blood. Therefore shall the land mourn, and every one that dwelleth therein shall languish, with the beasts of the field, and with the fowls of heaven; yea, the fishes of the sea also shall be taken away" (Hosea 4:1-3). God judges the society that breaks these laws and ignores them. When the Old Testament is so clear on the matter of the right of private property, it is no wonder that among those who are attacking private enterprise there is such disdain for the Old Testament.

But the Sermon on the Mount, to which they constantly

refer, can give them little comfort. Jesus said: "Think not that I am come to destroy the law, or the prophets: I am not come to destroy, but to fulfil. For verily I say unto you, Till heaven and earth pass, one jot or one tittle shall in no wise pass from the law, till all be fulfilled. Whosoever therefore shall break one of these least commandments, and shall teach men so, he shall be called the least in the kingdom of heaven: but whosoever shall do and teach them, the same shall be called great in the kingdom of heaven" (Matt. 5:17-19).

Our Saviour again emphasizes the responsibility of private enterprise: "Therefore if thou bring thy gift to the altar, and there rememberest that thy brother hath ought against thee; leave there thy gift before the altar, and go thy way; first be reconciled to thy brother, and then come and offer thy gift" (vs. 23, 24). If you owe your brother anything, if you have not dealt squarely with your brother, if you have defrauded your brother, get those things straight, He tells us, before you come with a gift; and, He says, *Thy* gift"—private ownership.

Then the Saviour continues: "Agree with thine adversary quickly, whiles thou art in the way with him; lest at any time the adversary deliver thee to the judge, and the judge deliver thee to the officer, and thou be cast into prison. Verily I say unto thee, Thou shalt by no means come out thence, till thou hast paid the uttermost farthing" (vs. 25, 26).

In these two verses we have the whole social system in which we live. Men have rights. If we steal from a man, and we do not settle things privately, we may be haled before the judge.

Perhaps the most outstanding capitalistic verse, or, we might say, the verse that supports private enterprise as decisively as any we find in the New Testament, may be seen in Ephesians 4:28, "Let him that stole steal no more: but rather let him labour, working with his hands the thing which is good, that he may have to give to him that needeth." Thus, private property is protected. The use of that property to get gain in good causes is commended and commanded, and the whole scope of benevolences is opened up before the Christian—"to give to him that needeth." This corresponds to what our Saviour declared in the Sermon on the Mount, "Let your light so shine before men, that they may see your good works, and glorify your Father which is in heaven" (Matt. 5:16).

This, of course, leads us squarely into another proposition that ought to be set down and underscored. The Bible teaches and confirms the validity of what men today call the profit motive. Man works in order to gain—to gain food, to gain clothes, to gain a house for his family, to gain comforts and conveniences. All that is involved in the command, "Thou shalt not steal," protects and establishes the profit motive. The temptation to steal is the temptation to get property unlawfully or to get gain wrongfully. What we gain we should gain in accordance with God's command. This is the profit motive. So basic and fundamental is it to the Word of God that our Lord Jesus Christ used it in appealing to men in the greatest issue of all, "For what shall it profit a man, if he shall gain the whole world, and lose his own soul?" (Mark 8:36.) The appeal is vital. A man should seek to save his soul as the greatest profit imaginable. It is in the inherent tyranny of the economically controlled and planned society that man's soul is crushed.

Solomon, the wisest man of all, declared, "In all labour there is profit. . . . The crown of the wise is their riches: but the foolishness of fools is folly" (Prov. 14:23, 24). A fool and his money soon part. Again, "Wealth gotten by vanity shall be diminished: but he that gathereth by labour shall increase" (chap. 13:11).

The validity of the profit motive is no more strongly supported than in a striking parable told by our Lord. It is the profit motive that is the whole basis of the parable's point. "A certain nobleman went into a far country to receive for himself a kingdom. . . . And he called his ten servants, and delivered them ten pounds, and said unto them, Occupy till I come. . . . And it came to pass, that when he was returned, having received the kingdom, then he commanded these servants to be called unto him, to whom he had given the money, that he might know how much every man had gained by trading" (Luke 19:12-15). Here is private enterprise, the profit motive.

"Then came the first, saying, Lord, thy pound hath gained ten pounds. And he said unto him, Well, thou good servant" (vs. 16, 17). He brought the fruit of his gain which was ten pounds. He was commended for his enterprise and trading. Then he was rewarded proportionately, "Because thou hast been faithful in a very little, have thou authority over ten cities" (v. 17)—personal, individual reward for his efforts.

"And the second came, saying, Lord, thy pound hath gained five pounds. And he said likewise to him, Be thou also over five cities" (vs. 18, 19). He brought the fruits of his gain and received a proportionate reward.

The climax and tragedy of the story, however, comes in the treatment of the man who refused to involve himself in enterprise or to exercise, in any way, the profit motive. "And another came, saying, Lord, behold, here is thy pound, which I have kept laid up in a napkin: for I feared thee, because thou art an austere man: thou takest up that thou layedst not down, and reapest that thou didst not sow" (vs. 20, 21). The man was afraid of competition. He was afraid lest, when he went out into the world to risk (My, what an anti-social word that is today!)—to risk his pound in the market, he would lose it and have nothing left to show.

In a world of competition, one had gone forth and gained ten pounds. Another had gone forth and gained five pounds. Both received the fruits of their labors. Here is the man who refused to go forth into the market, and our Saviour declared, "Out of thine own mouth will I judge thee, thou wicked servant" (v. 22). When you listen to most preachers today, you are led to think that the wicked man is the one who goes out to profit! Our Saviour continued, "Thou knewest that I was an austere man, taking up that I laid not down, and reaping that I did not sow: wherefore then gavest not thou my money into the bank, that at my coming I might have required mine own with usury [interest, profit!]?" (vs. 22, 23.)

There is a tremendous responsibility in owning anything. God gave to these servants the talents. They used them as their own and reaped the fruits of their profit. Yet God reminded them that they were primarily His. But Jesus continued in His condemnation, "Take from him the pound, and give it to him that hath ten pounds. (And they said unto him, Lord, he hath ten pounds.) For I say unto you, That unto every one which hath shall be given; and from him that hath not, even that he hath shall be taken away from him" (vs. 24-26). The responsibility of men to work and to profit could not be set forth in greater contrast or with more powerful emphasis. Many people have not today because they could not use what was given them, or they misused what they had.

The same principles that we have just seen in the parable

from Luke are emphasized in a slightly different setting in Matthew 25 in the parable of the talents.

The command, "Thou shalt not steal," protects us in our monies and properties in order that we may use them before God for the blessing of ourselves and our fellow men. The profit motive is legitimate. It is not sinful in itself. It is, of course, set forth in the Scriptures in contrast to selfishness, and this is one reason why it is so easy to mislead people by trying to identify the two. It is also set forth in the Scriptures in contrast to covetousness.

The desire to use our properties for gain, for the advancement of the interests of our families and the human race, is not of the same substance as covetousness. The profit motive, in other words, is controlled by the commands of God's Word. To get profit by stealing is sinful and wrong, but to get profit by honest, truthful, and honorable means is right. Therefore, to condemn the profit motive in itself, per se, is the thing that is so wrong and that is, as we shall endeavor to point out in our factual presentation later, at the very heart of the whole divergence of the modern church from the historic position of the Scriptures and the church.

The realities of all that the Scriptures teach concerning stewardship confirm and establish the lawfulness of private enterprise. This is our third point. "What hast thou that thou didst not receive?" Everything that a man has he has been given by God—his soul, his body, his property. In the use of all these he is responsible to God. God owns them. God has lent them to him. "It is required in stewards, that a man be found faithful" (1 Cor. 4:2). Thus with private enterprise, with property, goes responsibility, and that responsibility is to a far greater and far higher power than any community or state, as in the collectivistic systems. It is the responsibility to the living God!

Jesus Christ emphasizes these things in what is popularly called the Parable of the Rich Fool, recorded for us in Luke 12, beginning with verse 16, "The ground of a certain rich man brought forth plentifully." He built his barns and stored his goods. "But God said unto him, Thou fool, this night thy soul shall be required of thee: then whose shall those things be, which thou hast provided?" The man forgot his stewardship, forgot that God owns all that he possessed.

It is in this field of stewardship that private enterprise has exposed itself to all the charges that have been made against it. It is because of the sins and failures of private enterprise in the field of stewardship that the attack now being made upon it is possible, an attack that does not stop just with the correction of the abuses, but an attack that goes on to the destruction of the very existence of the profit motive.

The Apostle James gives us the picture that ensues when stewardship collapses: "Go to now, ye rich men, weep and howl for your miseries that shall come upon you. Your riches are corrupted, and your garments are motheaten. Your gold and silver is cankered; and the rust of them shall be a witness against you, and shall eat your flesh as it were fire. Ye have heaped treasure together for the last days" (Jas. 5:1-3). The intimation is, of course, that the rich men have taken their treasures and stored them, not used them for the blessing of humanity. Then James continues, and declares that there is much more involved. Their gain, some of it, had been secured by fraud. "Behold, the hire of the labourers who have reaped down your fields, which is of you kept back by fraud, crieth: and the cries of them which have reaped are entered into the ears of the Lord of sabaoth" (v. 4).

It is here that the church of Jesus Christ in all its authority and with all the force of the Ten Commandments behind it should lift up its voice today and speak to the capitalists, speak to the men of private enterprise, speak to men everywhere, and hold up before them their responsibility to society and to their fellow men. Benevolence is the word. In that capitalistic verse in Ephesians, Paul said that we are to labor at that which is good in order that we may have to give to them who have need. It is the fountain of giving that is drying up, that has dried up.

Of course, as we move on into a planned or controlled society where the Government is responsible for the poor and needy, then those who have means are not going to give. They will let the Government fulfill that responsibility. Just here appear in the foundation of our present social order the great fissures that have been created by the explosion touched off by those who are trying to change the very basis of society. There is not the slightest intimation in the Parable of the Rich Fool, to which we have referred, that the possessions were not his to use, or that the enterprise by which he secured them was wrong. He had the wrong attitude toward what he had gained; consequently, he made the wrong use of it. Free society *has* to exist with free benevolence. When free benevolence dries up, free society is soon at an end. Men today are prone to blame the drying up of benevolence on the control of society, but that is not the case. It is the other way.

There is, finally, revealed in the Scriptures, a fourth field of truth which emphasizes the validity of private enterprise and its place in society. It is what we call freedom of conscience. If men are to have free consciences, they must be free to use their means and direct the affairs of their lives, not by any compulsion from a group or from the State. "So then every one of us shall give account of himself to

God" (Rom. 14:12). Again we are told, "Ye are bought with a price; be not ye the servants of men" (1 Cor. 7:23).

Here, of course, we have the Scriptural basis for the realities of democracy. Each man is free to vote as he believes God wants him to vote. Individual freedom and democracy go hand in hand. Control the economic life of an individual, and you destroy his freedom, for that is what his material and physical life is. It is economical—his property, his food, his clothes, his pleasures, his money. It is the use and interplay of these things in human society that men call the economical. But if a man's economic life is controlled by the group—and a man's place in it is determined by the group—then how can that man render an account of himself to God? In a controlled society, the control of which is determined by others and not by himself individually, he cannot render an account of himself. He could say to God, "Lord, You know I want to render an account of my conscience to You, but I cannot. All my affairs are determined by the majority vote. I cannot do with them what I want to do or what I think I ought to do, so please excuse me, Lord; and blame the majority." A man must be free to be the minority or there is no freedom. Men have to have clear consciences, or there are misery and death.

The Apostle Paul emphasized this truth in 2 Corinthians 1:12: "For our rejoicing is this, the testimony of our conscience, that in simplicity and godly sincerity, not with fleshly wisdom, but by the grace of God, we have had our conversation in the world, and more abundantly to youward."

There are millions of individuals upon the earth. No two individuals are alike. The circumstances of no two individuals are alike, and each individual has the rsponsibility of applying the truth of God, as he sees it, to his own personal circumstances. He alone can do it, and he does it in the knowledge that God knows everything that he thinks. Here we have the reality of private initiative and individual freedom. They cannot exist unless we have a free society, uncontrolled, unplanned for the individual by the State or by the group. The controlled society, whether it be nazi, fascist, communist, socialist, is a blow at liberty of conscience, and, if the conscience be not free, the individual is not free. If the individual be not free, then we do not have a free society.

After I had planned the outline for this story, I secured a copy of "The Road to Serfdom," by Friedrich A. Hayek. In his volume, which every American ought to read, Dr. Hayek, from the economic and intellectual standpoint, defends the position of the individual. He does it purely from an intellectual vantage point. He analyzes the condition of the free individual in every relation to society, and also in a controlled and planned order. His logic is devastating; he does not, however, in regard to these questions, approach the problem in the light of Scripture, nor does he in any way mention the matter of the authority of the Scriptures or the position of God's Word. He naturally would not be expected to do so. However, there is one point in his analysis where he does touch upon this question of freedom of conscience. This is the nearest he comes to the level or the nature of the approach that we are endeavoring to make here.

In a chapter entitled, "Why the Worst Get on Top," he has this to say:

"Every collectivist system . . . does not leave the individual conscience free to apply its own rules and does not even know any general rules which the individual is required or allowed to observe in all circumstances. This makes collectivist morals so different from what we have known as morals that we find it difficult to discover any principle in them, which they nevertheless possess" (p. 146).

Any system that destroys freedom of conscience is immoral and is based on an entirely different system of morals—pagan, and may we say, atheistic morals. We shall discuss this matter further in an entire chapter.

Professor Hayek's book is having a salutary effect in England and America, and we were interested to observe that Dr. Paul Hutchinson, a modernist preacher, in a review of "The Road to Serfdom," in the *Christian Century* for January 3, 1945, declared that the book had profoundly disturbed him. Dr. Hutchinson explained that he had more or less taken it for granted that we were moving on into a socialistically controlled order.

It is the teaching of the Bible, as we have summarized it, that gives morality, stability, and foundation to society; and it is into the reality of this emphasis upon the individual that the State must not enter. The State must leave the individual free. The State is to serve as a punisher of evildoers, murderers, robbers, thieves, and the like. The Ten Commandments underlie the social order and limit the sphere of the State's authority and power. It is more than significant that the Ten Commandments do not have in them a single word that refers directly to the State. The State derives its authority from God. In the light of the commands of God, the free society is God's. It is therefore the duty of the State, as the minister of God for righteousness (Rom. 13), to see that this free society of competition, private enterprise, is preserved.

When individuals join, forming monopolies and establishing controls which hinder the flow of individual enterprise and initiative, the State has a responsibility to step in and say, "The log jam must be opened." In this respect the State may become a policeman or a governor to see that the ordered liberties of the people in the society are not transgressed but maintained. The only restraints imposed by the Government upon a free society are the restraints that will keep society free. As long as society is made up of individuals—and that is the only kind of society we shall ever have on this earth—the rights and liberties of each must be protected and guarded.

This stands in violent contrast to the so-called planned economy or social control of the economic processes for the common good. This free enterprise is not chaos. It is ordered; its freedom, in the very nature of things, has been created by the living God.

God created this world. God made the circumstances and conditions. God placed men in it, and it is God's order that gives us this freedom. If men want their own "planned economy," then they, of necessity, must break with the free order God has established.

God planned in a very particular way. Not only did He create this order, but He is also active in it. When the Psalmist said, "The Lord is my shepherd; I shall not want," he was depending upon the activity of God to provide for us. God is in free economy. He is in all the elements that men call chance. He is in all the factors that men call "fate." The Christian sees Him there. The Christian recognizes Him there when he says: "All things work together for good to them that love God, to them who are the called according to his purpose" (Rom. 8:28).

For this reason the genuine Christian must rise up and

oppose with all his might a controlled and planned economy where either a group of men or a majority of the people, through what may be called economic democracy or industrial democracy, seek to impose their order upon the society for what they think is the common good. The greatest thing that God has given to us in our society is liberty. This liberty is in His law, His Word, as we have sought briefly to summarize and point out.

CHAPTER 3

THE APPEAL OF THE COLLECTIVIST

ONE cannot make an appeal to the Scriptures, as we have done in the previous chapter, and claim their warrant and authority for the position we are defending and advocating, without recognizing that the opposition also appeals to the Scriptures. Those who are attacking private enterprise and pushing the individual out of his place and security, as given to him in the Bible, also appeal to the Bible. They find in the Bible—at least, they think they find in the Bible—support for their planning and their control of the economic processes. They find in the Bible—at least, they think they find in the Bible—texts from which to preach their gospel of the submerging of the good of the individual for the greatest good of all. Naturally, this emphasizes the seriousness of the situation.

We have appealed to the Bible in the previous chapter in order to establish the truth. Their appeal to the Bible is also made with the purpose of establishing the truth of the position they are advocating, and also of gaining entrance into the hearts and minds of people.

If one can make people think that the Bible is on his side, he has gone a long way in winning the battle. This is the situation in this land of ours, where a generation has grown up within the sound of the Bible. It is this appeal to the Scriptures on the part of those who are advocating their various collectivistic forms of society that has actually misled many sound Christian businessmen. They honestly think that the private enterprise system is inherently wrong, that other motives should be substituted for the profit motive, and that we should establish a system where competition is at an end or at a minimum.

Those who are attacking our system of private enterprise have their Scripture texts on the tips of their tongues, and, because the rest of us have taken our system for granted, we are not so well prepared to answer them or to refute them. Consequently, they get the best of the argument as they advance on the road to destroy or replace the present social order with the utopia that will come when we have finally conquered and controlled the economic problems by establishing our "economic democracy."

The most outstanding and prominent passage is, without doubt, the account of the action of the early church in Jerusalem, as given in Acts 4:32 to 5:11. "And the multitude of them that believed were of one heart and of one soul: neither said any of them that ought of the things which he possessed was his own; but they had all things common." Dr. E. Stanley Jones, Methodist leader, used this passage as the thesis of one of his books, "The Choice Before Us." It is the principle, he says, which is recognized here that must become the principle of the kingdom of God. Dr. Jones declared:

"Unless spiritual unity is founded in an economic and social unity it will go to pieces. These people in the early Christian society naturally and normally saw that the spiritual unity could not be kept apart from economic and social unity. They refused to departmentalize their unity. Life was one. If they were one in purpose, they would be one in purse. They would have their own personal possessions, such as clothing and every private thing; but the means of living were in the hands of all for the good of all. The result was the Christian cooperative order" (p. 55).

Dr. Jones recognizes, of course, that this particular plan failed. It never was put into operation later in the church; but his explanation of this shows how tremendously important the passage is in the whole setup of the kingdom which he advocates:

> "It was a cooperative order in consumption, not in production, and because it was thus only partially applied it failed, as it was bound to do with this partial application" (p. 57).

If the ideal church should have gone on into this kind of social order, it is strange indeed that the Apostle Paul in his epistles did not instruct us to do so. The epistles nowhere indicate that the "kingdom of God" involves this common ownership of all the means of production for the good of all. This is a very slender thread on which to build the kingdom of God, a social order in which all the means of production will be in the hands of everyone for the good of all.

No, this experiment failed because it was an extreme; it was wrong. Christians today bring their offerings and put them in a common purse to be distributed among the needy in the congregation, to each according to his need. There is nothing wrong with that. But, these first Christians brought all they had. There was an agreement in regard to this collectivism, and it was this principle of collectivism that produced the liar and the dead, and then the fear that fell upon all the people (Acts 5:11), and caused them rightly to abandon the experiment.

Paul gives us another verse equally as decisive as the one we have quoted previously from Ephesians 4:28. He does not give any encouragement to a Christian to wait, to sit around, to hope that the community, out of its common purse, will provide for him. "But if any provide not for his own, and specially for those of his own house, he hath denied the faith, and is worse than an infidel" (1 Tim. 5:8). "If any would not work, neither should he eat" (2 Thess. 3:10). If a man is not ready and willing to do the best he can with what he has, he should be given no material help. He should, however, be given some exhortation.

A short time ago one of the members of my church came to me at the close of a service with a letter in her hand. She was obviously distressed and disturbed, and asked me to help her. "I have a letter from my brother," she declared, as she unfolded it and handed it to me. "He has some of these communistic ideas," she added. I began to read the letter.

"I could quote a dozen passages that should leave no doubt in your mind," he wrote, meaning passages of the Bible which would support the communistic idea, "but one or two will suffice. Do you remember when Christ spent the night with the master of a vineyard, when He saw the servant trampling the juice from the grapes and the winefat? He said the pay of the servant and the pay of the master should be the same. At another time He told the parable of the reapers to illustrate the same thing. One worked all day, another a few hours, another but one hour. He said they should all be paid the same. He does recognize that the ability of different people to work or produce varies vastly, but that their material needs are all the same. Your fear of giving up some of your liberty and achieving just shows you have been reading newspaper propaganda regarding it. Even if it were true that you would have to surrender some particular freedom in achieving equal justice for all, does not Christ say that the servant of all shall be master of all?"

Here was an appeal to the Scriptures, the kind of appeal that we hear day after day as we talk with men and women. It is in this way that effective, substantial work for really changing our social order is done. Is there any justification whatsoever in these passages to which reference is made, and are there "a dozen passages that should leave no doubt"?

Let us look at the three he mentions. In the first place, unfortunately, so far as his argument is concerned, I cannot find the passage in the Bible to which his first reference is made. So much of the talk about the Bible's supporting socialism or communism or a planned social order is of this sort. The second reference which he says has the same principle as the first, which we could not find, is contained in Matthew 20. Does this support the principle of "from each according to his ability and to each according to his need," which is the communistic, collectivistic principle?

"For the kingdom of heaven is like unto a man that is an householder," said Jesus Christ, "which went out early in the morning to hire labourers into his vineyard." Here is a capitalist going out to hire men to work for him. Here is a man who is engaged in private enterprise going out and, by contract, engaging men to serve for the day. "And when he had agreed with the labourers"—here is your bargaining. It is more than just individual bargaining. The group he met first he apparently dealt with collectively. "And when he had agreed with the labourers for a penny a day, he sent them into his vineyard." Again we have private ownership —*his* vineyard. It was not a collectivistic farm.

The parable continues: "And he went out about the third

hour, and saw others standing idle in the marketplace, and said unto them; Go ye also into the vineyard, and whatsoever is right I will give you. And they went their way." There was no agreement made here; there was no contract into which they entered, other than that these labourers agreed to trust the good judgment of their employer.

"Again he went out about the sixth and ninth hour, and did likewise. And about the eleventh hour he went out, and found others standing idle, and saith unto them, Why stand ye here all the day idle? They say unto him, Because no man hath hired us." Here once more is private enterprise—going into the market and hiring laborers. But it should be observed that here, again, no agreement was made as to the amount to be paid for the day or for the hour. The master's agreement with these was, "Go ye also into the vineyard; and whatsoever is right, that shall ye receive." There they placed their labors in the hands of their employer, trusting that he would give them what was right. In the light of conditions today, it was rather a strange labor relationship.

Now let us see what happened when the evening came and it was time for the men to receive their wages. "So when even was come, the lord of the vineyard saith unto his steward, Call the labourers, and give them their hire, beginning from the last unto the first. And when they came that were hired about the eleventh hour, they received every man a penny. But when the first came, they supposed that they should have received more." They, of course, had heard, or had been informed by those who had received their wages previously, that they were getting a penny. Since they knew that these other laborers had come into the field later than they had, they thought perhaps they would get more, but they "likewise received every man a penny. And when they had received it, they murmured against the goodman of the house, saying, These last have wrought but one hour, and thou hast made them equal unto us, which have borne the burden and heat of the day."

It is here that the man who wrote the letter to his sister thought the communistic principle was expounded in the Scriptures. Nothing could be farther from the truth. The men who were employed in the earlier part of the day had signed a collective bargaining contract with the owner of the vineyard. That contract, to which they had agreed, gave them one penny a day. The others did not sign a contract. They simply agreed that whatever the master wanted to give them would be satisfactory to them. It is significant to notice the murmuring "against the goodman of the house." When men do not get paid in proportion to their labor, there is trouble. This ought to illustrate that the communistic principle of "from each according to his ability and to each according to his need" is unsound and full of trouble. The men who signed the contract, and were first to be employed, thought that, since they had worked longer, even though they were on a contractual basis, they ought to get more. In any planned or controlled society where men do not receive the fruits of their labors and an equal and proportionate pay for their time and ability there is going to be murmuring, infinitely more murmuring than there is under free enterprise.

The parable, however, clinches the answer. "But he [the master] answered one of them, and said, Friend, I do thee no wrong: didst not thou agree with me for a penny?" In effect, he said, "I have fulfilled the contract with you. What further complaint can there be?" "Take that thine is, and go thy way." In other words, "You have earned it; it is yours; you agreed to it. I owe you nothing more. Go your way."

"I will give unto this last, even as unto thee." Notice the word "give." He had promised to do right by these men who had come in at later hours and had trusted him to deal fairly with them. "Is it not lawful for me to do what I will with mine own?" Here is a man who owns his own vineyard—private enterprise—and it is lawful for him to do with his own what he will. Here is involved everything that we have emphasized in the previous chapter. "Is thine eye evil, because I am good?" He was good. The idea that all the leaders of private enterprise and industry are bad is not right. The real evil here was on the part of the first laborers. The men who signed their collective bargaining contracts did not come back with any further complaint.

I think it should be observed also that this vineyard was not a "closed shop." Other men were working there. If the shop had been "closed," so to speak, they would have had to deal with the men who had contracted for a penny, and paid them proportionately, as they demanded.

It is interesting to see, in the conflict of the present-day labor-management difficulties, all the elements involved in this parable. There is in reality nothing new under the sun. The attitude of the men who signed the contract and received less than the men who did not sign a contract, and their attendant murmurings, remind me of a difficulty of which we heard in a certain plant last Christmas.

The employees went on a strike because of a grievance of one particular individual. They were out over Christmas, and the matter was not settled until after New Year's. In previous years, before they had gotten their closed shop, these employees had received the wages they are receiving today, and it had always been the practice of the management to give every man a large turkey as a Christmas gift. Naturally, being on strike over Christmas, they did not get the turkey. When the agreement was settled, and they came back after the first of the year, they then decided to go on a strike in order to force the management to give them a turkey. "Is thine eye evil, because I am good?"

The more cordial and confident relation of the men who went in later and left the amount of wages to the good judgment of the employer in whom they had faith actually got them more than the others. It usually will—with a fair-minded employer.

This parable, instead of establishing the communistic principle, recognizes the right of private ownership, the right of the manager of an establishment to enter into contract with his laborers and also to give and do as he pleases with what is his. In the onslaught upon private enterprise today, with the extremes that are coming into labor as a result of the leadership of the church, it is no wonder that men are crying out, "My business is not my own." "Is it not lawful for me to do what I will with mine own?"

The third passage referred to in the foregoing letter was a reference to a very familiar text in the Gospel according to Mark: "But so shall it not be among you: but whosoever will be great among you, shall be your minister: and whosoever of you will be the chiefest, shall be servant of all. For even the Son of man came not to be ministered unto, but to minister, and to give his life a ransom for many" (Mark 10:43-45).

The appeal here made to the words of our Lord Jesus Christ is the basis for the individual's being willing to give up certain of his liberties and conform to the place which he might have in a planned economic or communistic order.

It is even suggested that we might have to give up certain liberties and that we should be willing to do so to obtain the end desired. Nothing could be farther from the spirit of the Bible. We are to stand fast in the liberty wherewith Christ has made us free; we are not to be entangled again in any yoke of bondage. This applies with equal force to the Christian life and also to the Christian's social relationships. Christ does not mean by these words in Mark 10 that he who would be first among you should become a slave or be willing to join in an order in which all would be actual slaves to the rulings of the planners. Nothing could be farther from the meaning of the text. It suggests a life of service, a life of sacrifice, a life of humility, living for others in a free world. A man must be free in order to live such a life. It does not mean that private enterprise must be destroyed or that the free competitive social order in which we now live should be replaced by some other kind of order.

But this text goes much deeper. It gives us the example, in this setting, of the Son of man giving His life a ransom for many. Jesus Christ did not submit Himself to being a slave. He offered Himself a sacrifice for the sins of the race, something that no other man could ever do. As the sinless, spotless Lamb of God He made an atonement for the iniquities of men, and in that atonement He has made possible liberty and life. It is because of His atonement, and the liberty and life which He provided for men, that men desire the freedom of enterprise, the freedom which God's Word demands.

This text, of course, emphasizes that there are more valuable things in the world than money and possessions. A life of service is a happy life, even though the person who lives it may not have very much of this world's goods. The idea that we should willingly and freely give up the life that is provided to men in the freedom of enterprise, and accept the restraints of a controlled society could not possibly be the meaning of this passage. If it were, we should all voluntarily become slaves. We could easily have done this by surrendering to Hitler, thus avoiding war and saving many lives! Think of the good we could have done by such an act of sacrifice!

It may be said that there are other passages that we should mention, but we have given here the main ones, all from the New Testament, and have pointed out that, instead of their supporting the communistic idea, they support the idea of the individual. It is the individual who makes the decision to spend his life in the service of humanity, in the task of making other people happy, and this can be done only in a free society.

There are, however, a number of phrases taken from the Scriptures that are slogan phrases used by the leaders of the Federal Council in their drive to win the assent of Christian people everywhere to the planned economy. One of these is "brotherhood." We feel that it would be better to speak of these later, after we have brought the evidence that proves the case which we have alleged, and in the light of which proof our discussion will be much more meaningful.

The appeal of the collectivist to the Bible is a false appeal, but because so many people are ignorant of the Bible, they are unable to discern these false arguments. If private enterprise be destroyed and liberties be taken from us, ignorance of the Bible will constitute the most determining factor.

Horace Greeley stated it so emphatically: "Liberty cannot be established without morality, nor morality without faith. It is impossible to enslave, mentally or morally, a Bible-reading people. The principles of the Bible are the groundwork of human freedom."

CHAPTER 4

THE WISDOM OF SOLOMON

THERE is a richness, there is a fullness, there is a depth to free enterprise; there is character; there is personality. There is the fullest possible development of the human spirit in a free economy. Before we leave this matter of appeal to the Scriptures, it will widen our appreciation of private enterprise and help us to see the depths of iniquity and the nature of the multiplied tyrannies that are inherent in a planned economy, if we study a little more closely what the Bible teaches concerning private enterprise.

This teaching is given for us in many of the practical sections of the epistles, as they express to us the development of the Christian life. However, there is one book in the Bible, the Book of Proverbs, that contains in condensed and varied form these values and verities.

Solomon, you remember, was given an opportunity to make a choice as to what he wanted—riches or power; and he asked God to give him wisdom. God gave it to him, and also He gave him both wealth and power; Solomon, in turn, has given to the world the legacy of these proverbs. There is nothing like them in all the literature of the ancients. There is nothing to compare with them in any work that man can name. They are inspired; they wholly support the private enterprise system—free and uncontrolled economy. In no other system could the demands made in these proverbs be realized or even partially appreciated.

"Honour the Lord with thy substance, and with the first-fruits of all thine increase" (Prov. 3:9). This recognizes private property and the responsibility to God, who gave it. "All thine increase" means all profit or gain. The gaining of profit from your substance is legitimate. This proverb carries the promise that if the individual—and it is to the individual that the proverb is addressed—uses his substance and his gain in the way indicated, "so shall thy barns be filled with plenty, and thy presses shall burst out with new wine" (Prov. 3:10).

"There is treasure to be desired and oil in the dwelling of the wise; but a foolish man spendeth it up" (Prov. 21:20). In other words, a man has a responsibility to protect and keep what he has for his use and dwelling. This is another aspect of the profit motive. The word "desired" goes to the very heart of the whole profit incentive. Such treasure is to be desired. It is not sinful to desire it. On the other hand, the foolish or sinful man is the one who spends it.

"House and riches are the inheritance of fathers: and a prudent wife is from the Lord" (Prov. 19:14). There is nothing wrong with desiring to help our children prosper; the ownership of our houses we may pass on in an inheritance to our children. The one place today where the whole onslaught upon the private enterprise or capitalistic system comes into focus may be seen in the attacks that are made upon the general idea of an inheritance. It is wrong, men tell us, for children to inherit anything from their parents. Instead of leaving their possessions to their children, the parents should leave their possessions to the State "for the good of all." But these texts that we have just quoted recognize the individual's right to use his property and to give it away. We shall have more to say at the end of this chapter about this reference to the wife. She is important, and her prudence is precious.

There are other proverbs that emphasize that profit is

secured by hard labor and good judgment. "Wealth gotten by vanity shall be diminished: but he that gathereth by labour shall increase" (Prov. 13:11). "He that gathereth in summer is a wise son: but he that sleepeth in harvest is a son that causeth shame" (Prov. 10:5). "A man shall be satisfied with good by the fruit of his mouth: and the recompence of a man's hands shall be rendered unto him" (Prov. 12:14). A man has the right to enjoy the fruits of his own labor. In the reference to the son's causing shame, we have opened up before us the field of character, the good name of the family. Those who condemn the profit system, because it gives honor to those who gain, forget that the Bible teaches that those who are slothful, careless, and wasteful bring shame and dishonor to the family name. They lose their possessions. Because the temptation to be slothful is ever present in the weakness of the human flesh, Solomon dwells upon this subject at great length in the Book of Proverbs. "The desire of the slothful killeth him; for his hands refuse to labour" (Prov. 21:25).

"He also that is slothful in his work is brother to him that is a great waster" (Prov. 18:9). This text approaches, from two angles, the matter of property and gain. A man who is slothful does not gain; a man who wastes what he possesses has no more than the slothful person. We often put it another way in our daily conversation—"A penny saved is a penny earned." This text places before us the idea of thrift, of self-reliance. "The slothful man roasteth not that which he took in hunting: but the substance of a diligent man is precious" (Prov. 12:27). The proper attitude toward private initiative and the exercise of the profit motive produces conservation of resources.

"Yet a little sleep, a little slumber, a little folding of the hands to sleep: so shall thy poverty come as one that travel-

leth, and thy want as an armed man" (Prov. 6:10, 11). There
is no truer saying than "God helps those who help themselves." Solomon had no patience with the slothful man. He
declared: "The slothful man saith, There is a lion in the
way; a lion is in the streets. As the door turneth upon his
hinges, so doth the slothful upon his bed. The slothful
hideth his hand in his bosom; it grieveth him to bring it
again to his mouth" (Prov. 26:13-15). In these passages Solomon recognizes the reality and validity of what we call the
competitive world of free enterprise. If a man is going to go
out and compete with others, he has to work, and in that
work there are many varied elements that enter into success.
It is the play and interplay of these elements upon the individual man that develop character and stability. "The way
of the slothful man is as an hedge of thorns" (Prov. 15:19).
Slothfulness begets all manner of trouble—lies, thefts.

"The sluggard will not plow by reason of the cold; therefore shall he beg in harvest, and have nothing" (Prov. 20:4).
The conclusion of this proverb is one of the roots from
which the whole profit enterprise system springs. In the free
field of private enterprise, the men who have gotten ahead
have had to plow even in the cold. They have sacrificed;
they have worked and slaved for the accomplishment of an
end which they believed would give them profit and also
vantage from which to serve and live.

There are so many angles to this problem of getting on
in the world, the world of freedom; but the big angle is that
the burden rests upon the individual. This is where Solomon puts it. The key to the whole problem is the individual.
"The simple believeth every word: but the prudent man
looketh well to his going" (Prov. 14:15). Here is the man
who reads the contract carefully before he signs it.

"He that loveth pleasure shall be a poor man: he that

loveth wine and oil shall not be rich" (Prov. 21:17). Those who are calling for a controlled economy and the redistribution of wealth are doing it in an hour when men are drinking intoxicating beverages as they never have before. Somebody always has to pay the bill, and in any controlled society where men contribute according to their ability, but receive according to their need, men's drinking and dissipation, stemming from their sinful hearts, break down the idealism of giving to men according to their needs, and become much more powerful factors. This alone will destroy the system.

If, in the throes of the greatest reverse of the Second World War, when the Germans broke through into what was called the Belgian Bulge, and when General Eisenhower pleaded for more equipment and ammunition from home, the power of drink was so great that it actually disrupted the production at home, what will it do in a planned economy? The Christmas and New Year's "hangover" of 1944 kept men out of work for days, held ships in the harbor of Philadelphia, and actually closed many of our war plants. This we know from firsthand testimony. Again I say, if this factor of human nature, its weakness for drink, obliterated the need of the boys who were dying in the front lines, how far will it go toward demoralizing society when everything is planned and men are given their material possessions according to their need? It is only in a free competitive economy that men can suffer the harm and judgment of their own sins with the least impairment and calamity to those about them. It is more than significant, however, to observe that among those who have joined in the clamor for a controlled society and a planned economy are the slothful and the sluggards. They think this will be another way by which they can get something for nothing.

The element of good judgment and wisdom entering into

the individual decision which men must constantly make in order to secure their welfare and maintain their good name is held before us in the wisdom of Solomon. "Poverty and shame shall be to him that refuseth instruction: but he that regardeth reproof shall be honoured" (Prov. 13:18). "Discretion shall preserve thee, understanding shall keep thee" (Prov. 2:11). "Ponder the path of thy feet, and let all thy ways be established" (Prov. 4:26). To get gain, to be preserved, to have our ways established are all ingredients of private enterprise and the profit motive. "Counsel in the heart of man is like deep water; but a man of understanding will draw it out" (Prov. 20:5).

One of the most essential ingredients of this wisdom and discretion is fair dealing, just weights. The desire for gain, the profit motive, is circumscribed by truth and honesty. To gain profit in other ways is sin, and incurs the displeasure of the living God. "A false balance is abomination to the Lord: but a just weight is his delight" (Prov. 11:1). "The integrity of the upright shall guide them: but the perverseness of transgressors shall destroy them" (Prov. 11:3). "Lying lips are abomination to the Lord: but they that deal truly are his delight" (Prov. 12:22). "A just weight and balance are the Lord's: all the weights of the bag are his work" (Prov. 16:11). In other words, He is the One who has established such things as weights and balances in His creation. And men, in their relationships with each other, must abide by these matters written in nature.

"The getting of treasures by a lying tongue is a vanity tossed to and fro of them that seek death. The robbery of the wicked shall destroy them; because they refuse to do judgment" (Prov. 21:6, 7). This clearly interjects what we might speak of as the God-factor into the society of men, and this factor operates fully in a free economy. God is in the providences; He is in the "acts of God" which come in storms and calamities. In the free competitive order, men turn to God when these factors enter into their welfare; but in a controlled economy which shall attempt to mitigate these factors, men shall cease to look to God, but will look to the State. Instead of cursing and damning God, they will curse and damn the State.

Before we move on to the further developments of the Book of Proverbs, we ought to observe one very significant fact. In the condemnation of the slothful, the sluggard, and in the emphasis upon the unwise judgment and the calamities that follow, there is not the slightest intimation that the profit motive is wrong, per se. There is not the slightest intimation that the free system of economy is wrong. It suffers; it is abused; individual men are crushed and suffer from it, but the system itself is not wrong. It is not the free enterprise system that produces these conditions. Rather it is certain individuals in it who produce the failure in their particular cases. To get rid of this failure, the collectivists or the socialists suggest that we merge the individual into the group, thus solving the problem. Instead, it only demoralizes the group and makes the individual more irresponsible.

Benevolence, or stewardship, which we discussed in Chapter 2, now comes to the fore in the Book of Proverbs. We cannot preserve the private enterprise system without it. Those who have made a success must help others who, through their own bad judgment or through calamities beyond their control, need to be helped. This kind of relief will stimulate the individual to help himself rather than to demoralize himself further as the collectivistic system does. Benevolences are the governor on the private enterprise system. If benevolences fail, the system will go amuck.

"Withhold not good from them to whom it is due, when

it is in the power of thine hand to do it. Say not unto thy neighbour, Go, and come again, and to morrow I will give; when thou hast it by thee" (Prov. 3:27, 28). Again, "He that despiseth his neighbour sinneth: but he that hath mercy on the poor, happy is he" (Prov. 14:21). "He that oppresseth the poor reproacheth his Maker: but he that honoureth him hath mercy on the poor" (Prov. 14:31). The concern of the rich for the poor is a responsibility that God has given to the rich by virtue of the wisdom and knowledge that He has given them in the gaining of their property. "He that hath a bountiful eye shall be blessed; for he giveth of his bread to the poor" (Prov. 22:9). "He that oppresseth the poor to increase his riches, and he that giveth to the rich, shall surely come to want" (Prov. 22:16). This is God's condemnation upon the exploiting about which we hear so much today and which is given as a reason why we must abandon the system of private enterprise for a collectivistic order.

"Rob not the poor, because he is poor: neither oppress the afflicted in the gate: for the Lord will plead their cause, and spoil the soul of those that spoiled them" (Prov. 22:22, 23). In times of great need, in times of calamity, it is the business of those who have this world's goods to come forth and help to deliver those who have not. This is benevolence.

One of the great fallacies of the present hour is that it is the Government's business to take care of the poor. The Government gets its money by the power of taxation. The Government thus dries up the wells of benevolence because a person is not going to give to the poor when he pays taxes which the Government collects for that purpose. When the Government takes over the responsibility of looking after the poor, then the Government takes over the responsibility of the regulation of the rich, and you are already several steps down the road that leads to a planned and controlled society.

The American Red Cross is one of the finest examples of what free men, independent of their Government, can do for the relief of the suffering and the needy. An agency such as this would have been infinitely better, from every possible angle, for the relief of the poor and the unemployed than the demoralizing shovel-leaning labors of the old W.P.A. and the disastrous favoritism of politicians. Public charities should be privately maintained and privately controlled! Had the Government given the contracts to private agencies, instead of setting up its own W.P.A., thousands of dollars could have been saved, and thousands more in need could have been employed!

The U.S.O., though we do not agree with all of its activities, is another example of what free enterprise can do.

But the system of free economy, the exercise of the profit motive, involves a great deal more than the free competitive order for men. It is in that system and under that plan that men are free to serve and to fear God. Good and honorable in itself, profit is not, in itself, an end. It is into this realm that Solomon now leads us. "Riches profit now in the day of wrath: but righteousness delivereth from death" (Prov. 11:4). "He that trusteth in his riches shall fall: but the righteous shall flourish as a branch" (Prov. 11:28). In other words, in the use and appreciation of the profit motive, men must realize that materialism is not the end of gain. "A good name is rather to be chosen than great riches, and loving favour rather than silver and gold" (Prov. 22:1). We have the two brought together in a very interesting verse: "By humility and the fear of the Lord are riches, and honour, and life" (Prov. 22:4). Riches and honor are set in contrast to poverty and shame. It is the honor and the shame that really

are the important things. "Better is little with the fear of
the Lord than great treasure and trouble therewith. Better
is a dinner of herbs where love is, than a stalled ox and
hatred therewith" (Prov. 15:16, 17). If, in our place, because
of our honesty, our profits are small, we must remember
what God says and a true conscience declares: "Better is a
little with righteousness than great revenues without right"
(Prov. 16:8).

There are other passages in the Book of Proverbs; the
whole book is packed with such statements on private enterprise, stewardship, benevolence. It stands out, for instance,
very clearly in passages referring to the fool. "Let a bear
robbed of her whelps meet a man, rather than a fool in his
folly" (Prov. 17:12). "A foolish son is the calamity of his
father" (Prov. 19:13). "The great God that formed all things
both rewardeth the fool, and rewardeth transgressors. As a
dog returneth to his vomit, so a fool returneth to his folly"
(Prov. 26:10, 11). Nowhere do we better see the force of all
that the Book of Proverbs gives us than in the conclusion:
"Every word of God is pure: he is a shield unto them that
put their trust in him. Add thou not unto his words, lest he
reprove thee, and thou be found a liar. Two things have I
required of thee; deny me them not before I die: remove
far from me vanity and lies: give me neither poverty nor
riches; feed me with food convenient for me: lest I be full,
and deny thee, and say, Who is the Lord? or lest I be poor,
and steal, and take the name of my God in vain" (Prov.
30:5-9).

The temptation of the rich is to be secure and self-
satisfied and to turn from God. The rich do not need Him.
They have made their profit. The temptation of the poor,
on the other hand, is to steal, to get gain by unlawful means,
and then to take the name of God in vain, to blame Him

for their calamity. In the midst of this competitive world, the writer declares that we want, in the gaining of profit, to be in such a place that we shall not be tempted to forsake the Lord, either on the right or on the left. If the element of risk is removed from society in the controlled and planned economy, men will not need to trust in the Lord or to look to Him for wisdom and guidance in the handling of their affairs. The group takes care of that.

Everything that has been said here about private enterprise, initiative, and responsibility is brought into a magnificent climax in Proverbs, Chapter 31, by its application to the virtuous woman. We spoke of her previously. After she is described in all her beauty and power, the last verse of Proverbs reads: "Give her of the fruit of her hands; and let her own works praise her in the gates." This is the reward of initiative, thrift, judgment, and the fear of the Lord. "Favour is deceitful, and beauty is vain: but a woman that feareth the Lord, she shall be praised" (Prov. 31:30). The character and riches necessary to build a home are the same as those necessary to build an estate or a life.

Before we turn from the Book of Proverbs, there are one or two matters that we should mention in order to protect ourselves from possible attack. That the Book of Proverbs supports private enterprise cannot be denied, but men may say that the Book of Proverbs does not apply to our complicated industrial life today. The philosophy involved here was applicable, of course, in the days of the sheep and the oxen, when life was simple; but in the multitude of competitors in our modern industrial era Solomon would have been as confused as anyone is today and would actually have advocated social planning!

In reply, it should be observed that the only reason

society has gotten so complicated and involved is because it is free. A planned society, if such were to be in existence, would work much better with just shepherds than it would if it attempted to correlate the innumerable contingencies and multiplicity of interests in our highly industrialized society. The only possible solution that can meet the problem of the complications is the individual in his personal position left free to exercise his judgment for his own profit.

The more fundamental answer, of course, is found in the declaration that what Solomon has given us is an enunciation of eternal principles and truth which abide.

We have studied carefully the Book of Proverbs, selected those proverbs that relate particularly to property and enterprise and have found various expressions of the different—may we say innumerable—angles of the command, "Thou shalt not steal."

Running through the same Book of Proverbs are mighty passages dealing with the command, "Thou shalt not commit adultery." "For by means of a whorish woman a man is brought to a piece of bread: and the adulteress will hunt for the precious life. Can a man take fire in his bosom, and his clothes not be burned?" (Prov. 6:26, 27.) No one would suggest for a moment that such proverbs do not have validity today.

Running through the Book of Proverbs, also, are injunctions dealing with the telling of the truth. Would anyone suggest that these proverbs have no validity? Yet, they are expressions in various forms of the great command not to bear false witness.

No, the entire Book of Proverbs is simply an exposition of the moral law. All of the Commandments are covered one way or another, and their validity is as eternal as God Himself. Societies based upon them will be free; and free men, realizing this, must fight for the realities of the profit motive, competition, risk, private enterprise.

We have endeavored to point out in this section that an appeal to authority is necessary, that this authority of the Scriptures supports the idea of free enterprise and a social order that is unplanned and uncontrolled economically. We have examined some of the passages that are alleged to support a controlled or a communistic social order; and then in detail we have explored the Book of Proverbs. No wonder men have spoken of the Bible as the Book of Liberty, for in all truth, "The entrance of thy words giveth light."

We shall turn now to examine, on the basis of evidence, the actual position of the modern church, the spokesman for the modern Protestant church, and the testimony of the larger groups within that body. It shall be our purpose to point out that they have departed from these principles and the ideas that we have here found in the Scriptures.

Part II

THE MODERN CHURCH

CHAPTER 5

THE VOICE OF THE CHURCH

THE constant cry in Protestantism for the last thirty years has been, "We need a united voice. The churches of the country should unite in bringing the impact of their witness upon the nation and the world." This theme has been emphasized so frequently that it scarcely needs any proof. It has been presented in various ways: too many denominations, too many creeds, too much competition, too much wasted effort, and the like. The visible evidence of this emphasis is known to almost every American—it is the Federal Council of the Churches of Christ in America. This body, a federal union of twenty-five denominations in the United States, actually claims to speak for the Protestant Church. It is, according to its own claim, and according to the recognition it has received in the nation, the voice of the church. It has used the appeal of being the voice of the church to persuade other denominations to join and strengthen this voice.

We were present at the meeting of the General Assembly of the Southern Presbyterian Church at Knoxville, in 1941, when that body voted to unite with the Federal Council. The telling argument used and re-emphasized over and over was that that church could not afford to remain outside of the influential organization that was the voice of the church; they should be a part of that voice and also help to mold that voice. They joined.

To appreciate the full force of the Federal Council's claim to be the voice of the church, we need only consider some of its own actions. In 1940, the executive committee of the Federal Council appointed a committee on appraisal—appraisal of itself—to determine "whether the available resources are now being used in the most advantageous way and for the most important objectives" (p. 28, Biennial Report, 1940). The report itself emphasizes the purpose and main emphasis of the Council.

"1. The organization of the Federal Council of the Churches of Christ in America in 1908 was the result of the converging influences of two predominant motives: first, the desire for a larger unity of the churches themselves, a unity based not merely on the voluntary coöperation of individuals and functional groups in the churches (like the Y.M. and Y.W.C.A.'s), but based rather on the official sanction of the denominations as such. This desire, it was widely agreed, could express itself adequately only through a new corporate body created by ecclesiastical authority. This, it was felt, was necessary to 'manifest the essential oneness of the Christian churches of America in Jesus Christ' and 'the fellowship and catholic unity of the Christian Church.' (*Constitution*, Preamble, Objective I.)

"The second major motive was the conviction that only through such a body could the message and teaching of the churches be brought to bear upon the many new issues which were emerging from the economic, political and social changes of the times. These issues were becoming so difficult that purely traditional ways of dealing with them no longer availed. And they were too formidable for any one body of Christians, relying simply on its own strength, to approach effectively. Moreover, because these issues lay largely in the field of the ethical and social application of the Gospel, it was possible for the churches to unite in dealing with them without engaging in extended discussion of the theological differences which had been so largely responsible for the development of the various Christian bodies.

"The desire for larger Christian unity and the *desire to bring the message of the churches of Christ to bear upon moral and social issues through unified effort* were thus the dominant motives of those who created the Federal Council. These motives have given the work of the Council a certain distinctive character across the years. They have been responsible for the development of most of the services of the Council, and for the programs of its departments. After thirty years these motives are still very influential in the thought and action of the leaders of the Council and of its active supporting constituents" (p. 29).

This report tells us not only that we have an official representative of the churches, but also that its main emphasis is to speak for the church upon moral and social issues through united effort. This is the direction in which the Council has gone, and is going, and it is tremendously significant for the purposes of this exposition, for it is the content of the message of this voice that is so revolutionary. We are, therefore, dealing in this study with the main message—the major impact of its program. When we consider its social program and goal, we shall come to grips with its major citadel.

In the appraisal report (p. 30) there is a table entitled, "Relative Values of Federal Council Services," which was constructed as the result of a questionnaire that was sent to the executive committee and denominational leaders in the Federal Council. One of the types of service which the Federal Council renders and which is considered of "great" value is "Voice of the churches." After the tables are given, the report concludes,

"All told the evidence of these tables testifies strongly to the continuance of both of the Council's original major motives" (p. 31).

What evidence could be better than this?

The testimony that it is within the field of moral and social issues that the Council is speaking brings into even bolder relief the significance and importance of the actual message, the germ idea, which the Federal Council has been giving to the country.

What is this voice? It certainly is clear, at this point, that, whatever this voice is, it does speak for the great bulk of the Protestants of the United States, and that it therefore has whatever weight this significant fact might have in itself.

The approach of the Federal Council to the field of social ideals and the application of these ideals to the condition of the economic and social life of the country have been most careful and thoroughgoing. In 1932, the Council adopted what is popularly known as the Social Creed of the Churches. Dr. Benson Y. Landis, associate secretary of the Department of Research and Education of the Federal Council, has prepared a book entitled, "Religion and the Good Society." Concerning this Social Creed of the Churches, adopted by the Federal Council, Dr. Landis reports in a signed article entitled, "Protestantism," as follows:

"The most comprehensive and representative statement of social ideals ever declared by American Protestantism was that adopted unanimously at a full meeting of the representatives of churches who were members of the

Federal Council of the Churches of Christ in America held at Indianapolis, Ind., December, 1932" (p. 30).

This Social Creed Dr. Landis calls "The Comprehensive Statement." The first two planks in it set forth the very heart of the attack upon the system of private enterprise, as we find it in the Scriptures and as it has been practiced in the United States throughout our history. The first plank of the platform strikes directly at the root of the matter and attacks the profit motive. The second plank sets before us the whole picture of economic planning. These planks are as follows:

"The Churches Should Stand For:

"1. Practical application of the Christian principle of social well-being to the acquisition and use of wealth, subordination of speculation and the profit motive to the creative and cooperative spirit.

"2. Social planning and control of the credit and monetary systems and the economic processes for the common good."

In Dr. Landis' article, just before he gives "The Comprehensive Statement," he has this to say about the general trend in the Protestant churches on these social ideals:

"In broad terms, the ideals have called for more social ends and more social means to achieve those ends than have generally been recognized by the leaders of society in the United States. The ideals that declared for an extension of democracy to industry and economic life generally were a bold challenge to the prevailing individualism of American life. Consequently these ideals have been unpopular with the large majority of the economic leaders of the nation" (p. 29).

This statement by Dr. Landis was made in 1942, but the Federal Council itself, at the time it adopted unanimously these social ideals in 1932, realized the seriousness of the changes involved, for it had this to say:

"No one can contemplate the profound social changes involved in any successful carrying out of these Social Ideals without realizing that, while they would mean great advances in human welfare and happiness, they make unprecedented demands upon the intellectual and moral capacity both of individual leaders and of the whole people. The significance of these demands is the greater since the Ideals express not only religious opinion but aspirations and goals which are stirring the heart of the world.

"We may legitimately expect that the collective mind of the nation will be equal to the intellectual and administrative tasks involved, especially under the stress of critical social conditions, if the moral qualities required are present in sufficient power. What our people lack is neither material resources nor technical skill—these we have in superabundance—but a dedication to the common good, a courage and an unselfishness greater than are now manifest in American life" (pp. 32, 33).

In Plank No. 1 of the Social Creed the controversy with private enterprise is squarely joined. The profit motive is here attacked and pushed down into a subordinate position which actually destroys its place and merit in society. We shall see in a later chapter, when we study the literature produced by the leaders of the Federal Council, the attack upon private enterprise means just this. These leaders insist that the profit motive itself is inherently wrong. That this is involved in the statement of Social Ideals is clearly more than just implied, because the social control of the economic processes, as intimated in the second plank, eliminates the profit motive in any individual operation. This is the reason we have taken such pains in the first section of this study to point out, in the light of the Bible, that the profit motive is legitimate in itself, that it is the dominant rule and controlling motive for enterprise and the securing of gain for the materials of livelihood and comfort.

We are also told by the Federal Council in the 1932 Social Creed,

"The motive of service supplants the desire for gain," and "the principle of competition appears to be nothing more than a partly conventionalized embodiment of primeval selfishness . . . the supremacy of the motive of self-interest."

The following year, 1933, the Council declared:

"The Christian conscience can be satisfied with nothing less than the complete substitution of motives of mutual helpfulness and goodwill for the motive of private gain."

Private enterprise, private gain, must be replaced by these other motives. Competition, which is the very life of private enterprise, is the only theater in which the profit motive can live. We are told it is the "embodiment of primeval selfishness." Please note that we are told it is the principle of competition which is this "embodiment of primeval selfishness." This is an attack of the most serious nature upon the very foundation of our social structure as it has come to us out of the Ten Commandments. This is simply a plank out of the platform of the constitution of the Soviet Union. But it is more than that. It adopts the kernel of the Soviet philosophy in this bold attack upon the profit motive and competition.

The Constitution of the U.S.S.R. states it as follows:

"The socialist system of economy and the socialist ownership of the means and instruments of production firmly established as a result of the abolition of the capitalist system of economy, the abrogation of private ownership of the means and instruments of production and the abolition of the exploitation of man by man, constitute the economic foundation of the U.S.S.R." (Article 4, Chapter 1, The Organization of Society, of the Constitution of the Union of Soviet Socialist Republics).

Notice especially those words "firmly established." When the system of economy based upon the profit motive is destroyed, only then can the other system be firmly established!

Before we move on to consider the second point in the Social Creed, perhaps this is the place to point out a significant factor, or should we say the strategic weapon, in meeting the attack by the "voice of the church" upon our free economy. There are numerous people who think that the effective way to silence this attack upon the private enterprise system is to catalogue a list of the attainments of private enterprise and to announce, This is why we must have private enterprise! Such a defense, of course, has some merit, and many businessmen and even laboring men who see the real issues involved employ such a method. This is the method so frequently employed, for instance, by business groups when they talk to church leaders; but such an approach is far more useless than pouring water on a duck's back. These Federal Council leaders, as we shall point out when we look at some of their own writings, recognize that private enterprise has done significant things; and to enu-

merate these values does not satisfy them, because they have
cut from under the enterprise system the very idea on which
it exists, the profit motive. If we are going to meet their
attack, we must meet it right in the arena where the profit
motive struggles.

Because of this fact we have undertaken this thesis to
show, upon the authority of the Word of God, that the profit
motive is valid and that the attack upon it is an attack upon
our American way of life and upon the historic Christian
faith itself.

It is at this stage of our story that we begin to catch a
glimpse of the tremendous issues at stake and the mighty
conflict raging in the present-day modern church. Is the
modern church breaking with its own past and the "idea"
which gave our land liberty? That is the serious question.

Plank No. 2 in this platform of the Social Creed, of course,
sets before us an economically planned and controlled society. Society is to plan and control the economic processes
for the common good. Society, of course, is the group which
the Federal Council believes should establish the "economic
democracy." It is to do the planning and controlling. All
these things are to be done for what is called "the common
good." This second plank clearly makes the whole conception more communistic than that given in Plank No. 1. Tear
down the system built upon the profit motive and private
enterprise, and you may have any one of a number of other
systems take its place—fascism, nazism, socialism, communism. But Plank No. 2 seems to indicate clearly that the
social planning be done by the group. It is on the communistic order. The similarity of this to the platform of the
Soviet Union and its economic life is startling because it is
so congruous.

Article 11, Chapter I, of the Soviet Union's Constitution is as follows:

"The economic life of the U.S.S.R. is determined and directed by the state national economic plan with the aim of increasing the public wealth, of steadily improving the material conditions of the working people and raising their cultural level, of consolidating the independence of the U.S.S.R. and strengthening its defensive capacity."

Here is the state national economic plan—social, the group, the state planning. The words "is determined" mean that a particular plan, in contrast to other possible plans, is decided upon. The word "directed" means controlled. When you have the economic life determined, you no longer have free economic life. When you have the economic life directed by the state national economic plan, you no longer have private enterprise.

Article 2, Chapter I, of the Soviet Constitution emphasizes this matter so clearly:

"The Soviets of Working People's Deputies, which grew and attained strength as a result of the overthrow of the landlords and capitalists and the achievement of the dictatorship of the proletariat, constitute the political foundation of the U.S.S.R."

This states the issue just as the Federal Council platform states it. There must be first an overthrow of the landlords and the capitalists. There must be an overthrow of the system resting upon the profit motive. Then there must be the establishment or achievement of the dictatorship. No phrase fits the Federal Council's phrase, "planning and control," any better than "dictatorship of the proletariat." The proletariat, of course, is the social group, and the dictatorship is the "planning and control." And this, we are told, constitutes the political foundation. Economic control and political operation go hand in hand. They have to. This involves the attack upon property—private property.

In our introduction we referred to the editorial written by the editor of the Muskegon *Chronicle*. The title of this editorial was "Whose Is the Voice of 'The Church'?" The thing that alarmed and aroused him about the meeting in Cleveland, Ohio, January 15-19, 1945, conducted under the auspices of the Federal Council, was that, accompanying their recommendations in regard to the Dumbarton Oaks Proposals, they took occasion to attack the right of private property as an absolute freedom.

In our previous discussion we pointed out that the command, "Thou shalt not steal," gives the right of private property to men on the basis of the moral law and the authority of God. That right is an absolute right. It takes precedence over the right of the State. The Michigan editor sought to have the adopted statement amended and clarified in the interest of the system of free economy.

The section which the Federal Council adopted, dealing with the matter of private property, is as follows:

"The right of private property is not an absolute right but a right qualified by the public interest. Likewise freedom of enterprise does not imply absolute freedom but operation of enterprise consonant with the interest of the public and the welfare of the nation. In the use of property and in the operation of enterprise, therefore, the welfare of society should be given primary consideration. . . . We must ask our people to recognize that in order to supply these needs for all, many changes may be necessary in our economic practices. These changes will probably lie in the direction of a larger measure of social planning and control than characterized our prewar system."

Concerning this attack upon private property the editor said:

"That statement, manifestly, has no relationship to the purpose for which the Conference was called. It was lugged in by the heels. It is the kind that is being lugged in by the heels wherever conferences of churchmen are brought together, and that have been permitted to go unchallenged, usually, either because there was nobody present to challenge them, or nobody wanted to make himself personally obnoxious."

The amendment the Michigan editor proposed is as follows:

"While the growing complexity of modern civilization has increased the area in which private property is affected by a public interest, so that the rights of private ownership have been circumscribed by the conceded superiority of the claims of the public welfare, we shall at our peril lose sight of the fact that human liberty has, in every age of the world, found its major expression in recognition of the right of the individual citizen to the fruits of his own toil, energy, ability and initiative.

"Freedom of individual initiative in the economic realm goes hand in hand with human freedom in the political realm. The two are inseparable."

Then the editor tells us:

"That is the statement of a basic principle this editor proposed to put into the Conference declaration, to indicate to the vast membership of the Christian churches of America, voiceless at Cleveland, that the declaration as quoted above on the rights, or lack of rights, of private property were made with recognition also of the basic truth, that economic and human freedom go hand in hand."

The president of the Federal Council, Dr. G. Bromley Oxnam, publicly disapproved the amendment and expressed his hope that it would not be adopted. It was referred to the drafting committee of which Bishop Oxnam was the president and not heard of again. The discrediting of the profit motive and the insistence upon a socially controlled and planned economy are both attacks upon the right of private property, one from one angle and the other from the opposite angle. If the right of private property is not an absolute right, but one qualified by the public interest, then the social control of all property is perfectly lawful in the sight of God.

When we come to the section dealing with the historic Christian church, we shall see that the creeds of the churches, the historic creeds, tell us that the right of private property is an absolute right. If it is not, then the way is open for collective ownership which is essential to social control, planning, and direction. This is emphasized by the Soviet Union's Constitution in Article 6 of Chapter I:

"The land, its natural deposits, waters, forests, mills, factories, mines, rail, water and air transport, banks, post, telegraph and telephones, large state-organized agricultural enterprises (state farms, machine and tractor stations and the like) as well as municipal enterprises and the bulk of the dwelling houses in the cities and industrial localities, are state property, that is, belong to the whole people."

Here the whole people and their rights take precedence over the rights of any individual to own land, mills, factories, mines, etc.

The fact that the Federal Council realizes the import and the clear logic involved in this can be seen in another of its carefully prepared statements which was adopted at the time of its Social Creed in 1932 and which Dr. Landis quotes in "Religion and the Good Society" referred to previously:

"Industrial democracy is a goal comparable to that of political democracy. Both are relative terms. There is more than one way of making progress toward their realization. In one stage of development, cooperation through collective agreements between the representatives of management and of workers, counseled by technical experts, may be the most advantageous. Even in this elementary form of industrial relations, the right of workers to organize and to be represented by counsel or agents of their own free choice must be recognized as fundamental. In other stage, participation of workers in management may be possible and desirable; in another, workers might provide their own capital and assume full responsibility; in still another, the government might assume and exercise the powers of ownership, control, and management for the common good."

Here are the stages, step by step, in the unfolding of this principle of social control, or, as it is here called, "industrial democracy." This goal of industrial democracy goes through these various stages. The last stage given here is that "the government might assume and exercise the powers of ownership, control, and management for the common good." Here is the fulfillment of Plank No. 2 of the Social Creed—"social planning and control of the credit and monetary systems and the economic processes for the common good." This is Russia. This is what Stalin does. This is where planned economy ends.

The Labor Day messages of the Federal Council refer to this same idea in their appeal to the nation each September. The message, for instance, in 1929, clearly involved this whole conception when it declared:

"If democracy in government may be made the object of a crusade, the workers' demand for a voice in the control of their working life cannot be opposed consistently by those who profess a Christian ethical standard. . . . It is for employers who entertain a Christian purpose and who are consciously governed by a Christian standard of dealing with their employees to ascertain what is just and fair in the new demands of labor and to meet those demands before enforcement of them robs concession of any merit."

It is the Federal Council's appeal to labor, the labor groups, and the way in which this appeal is being made that is fraught with such terrific consequences for the country. A little later we shall have an entire chapter dealing with labor. Yet, just here, I might say that the Federal Council is leading the labor movement beyond the legitimate bounds to which it, within the structure of free enterprise, can safely go. It is doing this by inspiring labor to believe that the profit motive is wrong, that the rights of private property are relative.

The real subtlety of the Federal Council in its hold upon the labor movement can be seen in the further consideration of the Social Creed. I heard Mr. John G. Ramsay, Public Relations Representative, United Steel Workers of America of the C.I.O., when speaking before the Federal Council in

Pittsburgh on Thursday evening, November 30th, tell the Federal Council that the labor movement and the Federal Council stood together against the National Association of Manufacturers because the church and the labor movement had the "social vision."

This Social Creed of the Federal Council, however, has in it some good things. As one reads on down the list he finds, for instance, the items: "Abolition of child labor; adequate provision for the protection, education, spiritual nurture and wholesome recreation of every child"; "The right of employees and employers alike to organize for collective bargaining." And there are other things.

Now it should be very clearly and definitely understood that within the framework of the system of individual freedom and free economy there can be social advance and progress. The abolition of child labor is such a progress. Collective bargaining is an extension of the right of contract which is an essential and permanent ingredient of the private enterprise system. As society moves along, as complications have come through industrial developments, the one thing that society must make sure of is that the arena in which the profit motive is maintained, the arena of competition, the arena of private enterprise, is secured. Any matters of growth that do not restrict that field and destroy it may be within the bounds of legitimate social growth under the structure of free enterprise. That is a big field in itself. But what the Federal Council has done in this Social Creed, having included such matters as the abolition of child labor, is to move over to embrace the collectivistic idea and to destroy the place and power of the profit motive.

These social improvements are like rubbing salve upon the sick body, while the attack upon the profit motive and the advocating of social planning are like sticking a dagger into the very heart of the patient. Men, observing the kind doctor putting salve on the patient's body, are not detecting the fact that he is, at the same moment, pushing the fatal needle of poison into the heart of his victim. This ought to be sufficient answer to all those who say, "Hasn't the Federal Council done a lot of good? Isn't it making a lot of fine progress in a social way?" The answer is, No. These good and legitimate social advances are but the attractive Christmas wrappings about the box in which, in the name of the church, the gift of a collectivistic America is presented. Certainly we can have sound social advances without tying them to destructive social ideas.

This leads us inevitably to the question, What is the Federal Council's attitude toward freedom in this new society that it desires to set up? It is just here that the conflict between the private enterprise system and controlled economy comes into closest quarter. One of the planks in the Federal Council's Social Creed is:

"17. Recognition and maintenance of the rights and responsibilities of free speech, free assembly, and a free press; the encouragement of free communication of mind with mind as essential to the discovery of truth."

Here is the reality of the situation. If the society is controlled, it cannot be free. If the social economy is planned, it cannot be free. If there is to be no competition, there is a monopoly of the social group. There simply cannot be the same freedom in a controlled order that there is in a free society. Any talk about freedom in a planned society involves either a blindness, a misunderstanding, or, let us say, a concept of freedom that is entirely different from that freedom which exists in free enterprise. The freedom of the planned social economy is a freedom that is consonant with the plan. It certainly could never be a freedom to destroy the plan because that would destroy the State. The rights of the individual cannot possibly go that far in a controlled order.

Russia declares in her Constitution that freedom of speech, freedom of assembly, freedom of religion are assured; but they are meaningless, so far as our American conception of freedom is concerned.

The key to the problem comes when one realizes that, in order to maintain this plan, the minds of people must be guided. They must be led to see that the plan and the order are reasonable and right, that the means of access to that mind—the press, the assembly, the organs of propaganda—must be directed for the maintenance and the furtherance of the plan. For a newspaper to attempt the destruction of the plan would be nothing less than sabotage. It would be hostility to the "free" expression of the majority as they have established the plan.

There will be, for instance, what could be called "freedom of religion" for everyone, so long as the church does not preach that the social order itself, per se, is wrong; and that the control of the individual and the destruction of free enterprise are an iniquity. In our present free society the Federal Council and its leaders are at perfect liberty to call these matters, which are the very basis of our existence, sinful and selfish, and no one ever thinks about locking them up; but when their "free" society is established and those of us who believe in a different conception of freedom begin to lift our voices, it will be necessary to liquidate us in order to preserve their "freedom" of control. To them, our present competitive order is sinful; to us, their controlled order is sinful. In our free order, they are free to call the present order wrong, but once they establish their order, we would not be free to denounce it. These are the real contrasts.

We shall pursue this matter farther when we come to another chapter, because this question relates to the conception of God and explains why the socialistic republic of Russia has been atheistic.

The really radical principles, and such they are, that we have seen in the Federal Council's platform of the social creed find their expression in the drive of the Federal Council to take over the legitimate co-operatives and also to establish co-operatives which are destructive of the private enterprise system. In a true sense, a co-operative is only another name for a corporation. Individual farmers or other groups have a right, if they desire, to join together in such a corporation and carry on their marketing in order to meet the competition of larger concerns. The Federal Council, however, comes along and endorses "co-operatives" in order to use them as instruments for the destruction of private enterprise and the establishment of a co-operative order in which the profit motive, competition, and the other elements of a free society are no longer existent. The Federal Council calls it a system of "economic brotherhood." This differentiation is exceedingly important because thousands of loyal Americans who believe in private enterprise are in danger of being misled by deceptive propaganda on this very point, and, before they know it, being made a party in many ways to a system that will utterly destroy the thing in which they believe. Throughout our discussion we will use the word "co-operative," therefore, to describe the Federal Council's conception of it, for it is with that propaganda we are here dealing specifically.

The Federal Council in its Labor Day message of 1939 had this to say about the co-operatives:

"One of the hopeful signs of the times is the fact that

labor and farmers are discovering that they are consumers as well as producers. They are finding in the consumers' cooperative movement significant common ground with increasing benefits to both farmers and city workers. The freer exchange of farm and industrial products through consumers' cooperation offers at once a more abundant economic life to both groups and brings them together in what Dr. Toyohiko Kagawa has called a system of economic brotherhood.

"We would point out . . . that the basic need, not only of farmers and labor, but of all economic groups, including employers and consumers, is to develop a broad understanding, a sympathetic attitude, a mutual loyalty and a spirit of confidence and goodwill. The soundness of these fundamental principles of Christian brotherhood affords the only sure basis for democracy and offers the only hope of the economic adjustments necessary to a practical and material solution of the problems which now confront us."

The above statement contains the whole collectivistic philosophy, so deceptive in the Federal Council's propaganda. Legitimate co-operatives are not in the slightest against competition or the private enterprise system, but the ideas involved here become all-inclusive and utterly destroy the free competitive order. The Federal Council's leadership in this field is gaining momentum. It has set up a department under the title, "The Church and the Co-operatives," and has as its head an outstanding churchman, Dr. J. Henry Carpenter, head of the Brooklyn Federation of Churches, whose recent book published in 1944 we are going to discuss in our next chapter, a book in which he utterly and completely repudiates the idea of sound co-operatives and sub-

stitutes the concept of the collectivistic, communistic perversion of the idea.

Article 5 reads as follows:

"Socialist property in the U.S.S.R. exists either in the
form of state property (the possession of the whole people),
or in the form of cooperative and collective-farm property
(property of a collective farm or property of a cooperative
association)."

These co-operatives as they are developing in the United
States are, in principle, little units of Soviet Russia.

There is a great deal more evidence and material that
could be supplied, but surely we have given enough in this
presentation to establish beyond a scintilla of doubt that the
"voice of the church," the body which speaks for Protestantism in the United States, is standing before the nation,
speaking in the name of its tremendous constituency, and
asking us to replace the entire basis of our social system with
one that involves the idea current in Russia. The seriousness
and the magnitude of this situation are almost impossible
to grasp. It startles; it stuns. The facts we have just considered speak volumes and augur trouble and tyranny.

Can it be possible that the body, claiming to speak for the
Lord Jesus Christ and for the Protestant Church which has
given us a Protestant nation, is actually, at this particular
stage in our history, asking our nation to turn its back upon
private enterprise, the profit motive, and to embrace the
philosophy that is thoroughly collectivistic and totalitarian?
The answer is, Yes. And further, this is the main emphasis
and message of the "voice of the church." To call it tyranny
is a mild, soft word. It is out of such an ideology and condition that the dreadful tyrant not only can but also will arise.
His hand, at this stage, appears soft and kind.

CHAPTER 6

LEADERS OF THE REVOLUTION

THE world has been overturned. The foundations have been shaken in country after country. The spirit of change and revolution is in the air, so this is a particularly propitious hour in which to advance the attack upon the private enterprise system; and able leaders are arising from our own number to do this very deed.

These are days of tremendous reverses and mighty shock. We have endeavored, in our last chapter, to bring the very best possible evidence available to support the thesis that the "voice of the church" in America, if followed, will lead us into real catastrophe. The ideas embraced in the Federal Council's social program, as we have seen them in the last chapter, have received their place of prominence and power within the Federal Council because preachers believed in them. Leaders of denominations and churches are convinced that they are a part of the Gospel of Jesus Christ and that, by following them, we shall be able to bring in, or to establish, the kingdom of God on earth.

It is time now for us to turn to some of these individual men, see who they are, and what they are telling us we should do. It is perfectly fair to the Federal Council for us to take the men whom it has honored and elevated to places of leadership and office and examine their writings and present their position as one with which the Federal Council is not in conflict. Suffice it to say that the zeal of the Federal Council for these social ideals is such that in putting its emphasis upon them it has sought to give them the very finest possible embodiment in personality. As a result of this, the ablest men of the day are in the places of preferred leadership, advocating these social theories. The Federal Council is serious. It means business in regard to this matter of changing our social order from one of free economy to economic democracy. It is a holy crusade with them. The day of march has come!

There are those who have said that, of course, in times past, the Federal Council did have some radical ideas, but this has all been changed and there has been a modification or toning down of this emphasis. Nothing could be farther from the truth, and in this particular study we propose to consider the men who are now leaders and examine their most recent works, works which have been written within the last year and a half. The emphasis, the zeal, and the variety of books and propaganda that are pouring forth from the Federal Council's mill at this hour, through these leaders, only emphasize that they believe we now face the momentous hour of decision.

History is fluid. The mold that is to be set in the making of the peace may last a while. Because of this they are busier than a cranberry merchant. It is not a question of bringing these doctrines in by the heels. Every time they assemble they announce them and re-emphasize them and raise them in various forms and shapes. It is the mind of the people, the mind of the masses, that they must mold. As we shall point out, the type of propaganda they are using is the same kind that was used in the Soviet Union to bring about the revolution, the turning of the workingman against the capitalist. It is a class strife. Of course, it is not being made in the name of class strife; it is being made in the name of the elimination of class strife. According to Federal Council leaders, the way of eliminating it is by way of the utter destruction of the capitalist, the bringing into its being of the co-operative social order.

J. HENRY CARPENTER

In Pittsburgh, in November, 1944, at the meeting of the Federal Council, I found on the literature table an attractive volume entitled, "Peace through Co-operation," by J. Henry Carpenter, published by Harper and Brothers, $1.25. On the inside jacket we read this about Dr. Carpenter:

> "Dr. Carpenter is Executive Secretary of the Brooklyn Federation of Churches, Chairman of the Committee on Church and Co-operatives of the Federal Council of Churches, Chairman of the Tour Committee of the Co-operative League of the United States of America, New York correspondent of the *Christian Century*, and probably the best informed church leader on the Co-operative movement. In 1942 he was invited by the Chinese government to inspect and make an advisory report on China's expanding co-operative program."

I believe it would not be possible to find a better witness than Dr. Carpenter to testify, and this latest book, written in 1944, brings us very much up to date.

"Peace through Co-operation" is a commending title. Naturally, we all know that if we are going to live with people we must try to get along with them, co-operate with them, work with them. But that is not the idea of this book. In fact, Dr. Carpenter clearly rejects any such idea.

> "The word, co-operate, is highly elastic. It is used in a variety of senses," he tells us, "some of which are nearly polar to the use I have in mind. Hence I must labor further to make my own meaning, which I believe to be the true meaning, clear."

After dismissing the ordinary uses of the word "co-operatives," he declares:

"We must be specific, not vague and general. To my mind, we can only find *peace through co-operatives*. . . . Capitalism, as we have known it, is irreconcilable with an organized society motivated by the spirit of love. We cannot co-operate under a competitive and monopolistic capitalism. And we cannot want peace unless we intend to co-operate. Thus by short steps we are face to face with the system of co-operatives. The question, what is peace, ends in another, what are co-operatives?" (pp. 8, 9.)

Then it is that Dr. Carpenter makes a subtle attack upon the whole system of private enterprise. The profit motive he rejects entirely. The profit motive, he believes, is responsible for all the ills of modern civilization, and it is directly responsible for war. If we could get rid of the profit motive and substitute some other motive, we could eliminate our ills and find peace rather than war.

"Co-operatives are a system of the production and distribution of economic goods, for the creation and allocation of wealth. Their general purpose, therefore, is often identical with that of capitalism; some of the appurtenances and some of the machinery of co-operatives are indistinguishable from the machinery employed by capitalism. But the rational, the inner spirit, are wholly different" (p. 10).

It is indeed clear that Dr. Carpenter is striking at the very roots of the economic system upon which capitalism and private enterprise rest. He says:

"Our old-fashioned economists and rugged individualists teach that the profit motive is the dynamic of industry and business [and may we add, so does the Book of Proverbs]. But this profit motive obviously can only be felt by, and activate the chosen few: the few the enterprise belongs to. And in pursuing their purpose they must needs be ruthless, for to share equally and benevolently would imply renouncing the very purpose of their possessions. Thus capitalism cannot escape these evils which many capitalists are no longer inclined to deny, for those evils are but a necessary consequence of the evil principle on which the structure rests" (pp. 21, 22).

Here we have the heart of the whole issue. The profit motive, the inner spirit, they believe, is evil. It is an evil principle upon which the structure of our social order rests. But the Bible holds it up to us as a reality with which all men must reckon. Yet, Dr. Carpenter continues:

"Attempts to bridge the gulf between owner and worker, or producer and consumer, by various compromises and gratuities only widens it and hastens the disintegration of the entire system. Let the workingman or the farmer adopt the profit motive for themselves, and take seriously the rule of self-interest, and industrial or business chaos ensues. . . .

"The co-operative program essays to offset the evils of industrial society or unequal distribution of profit by attacking them at their source. It supplies a new motive for the world of work and merchandising. This new motive is co-operation. Men are engaged in a common undertaking: the highest executive and the most menial laborer, the farmer and the city dweller, are uniting in a mutual quest. The rift between owner and employee, between farmer and laborer, which all labor or farm legislation is designed to seal, never appears at all. Industry is an organism from its inception, and all members of the body share the same fortunes. In the economic household of co-operatives, master and servant participate alike in prosperity and in adversity" (p. 22).

Thus we have clearly the meaning of the words "peace through co-operatives." In these co-operative associations, nobody owns anything. Everybody owns everything. No private enterprise is possible, except the one enterprise of the social system, the application of the social control of the means and instruments of distribution for the common good. Of course, there is peace brought about by the destruction of the owner and by having the employees own everything. This is communism, the communal ownership. In giving an illustration of this principle, Dr. Carpenter tells us of the Pennsylvania Farm Bureau Co-operative which painted upon the side of its feed mill at Manheim the slogan, "Farmers have paid for many mills, but this one they really own." Here is the collectivistic principle. The principle of one man's owning a mill, another man's owning a little grocery store, another man's owning the drug store, another man's owning the hardware store—private enterprise—is utterly destroyed by these co-operatives where everybody owns the mill. This has been brought about by the destruction of the profit motive and the substitution of a "new spirit" called co-operation, or the co-operatives. To say that this is revolutionary is mild. It involves a complete change in our whole American way of life.

The attack upon the private enterprise system is continued in a number of different ways throughout Dr. Carpenter's book. There is a chapter entitled, "Co-operation or Chaos." It ought to be called, "Co-operation or Free Enterprise," because with the word "chaos" he describes what is

really the free enterprise system. When men get to the place
where they call a system of freedom a system of chaos, it is
time for us to wake up and examine what we are being told.
It is characteristic of those who are attacking the private
enterprise system to misrepresent it by such words as "chaos"
and "selfishness," as though, when men pursue the profit
motive they are doing it purely out of sinful, selfish endeavor. It is interesting also to observe that the well-known
terms of the Christian religion are here used to embody an
entirely different idea from that which is used in the Bible.

"We must be remade, we must be born again," Dr. Carpenter declares. "We must find new motives for our living"
(p. 80). And this new birth, as he speaks of it, is the adoption
of the co-operatives by men! But Dr. Carpenter makes it
even stronger. He declares,

"It is my conviction that one cannot be a Christian, if
we must function within a society where self-interest and
personal profit are the dynamic of industrial life" (p. 11).

He is beginning to drop his block busters upon us when he
says we cannot be Christians and live in our society where
personal profit is the dynamic!

Personal profit not only has been but also is the dynamic
of industrial life, and, as we have endeavored to point out,
there is nothing wrong with it, per se. But so far as saying
"that one cannot be a Christian, if we must function within
a society where self-interest and personal profit are the
dynamic," it is not a question of the particular society in
which a man functions that makes him a Christian. It is his
personal faith and relationship to the Lord Jesus Christ that
determines whether he is a Christian or not.

That Dr. Carpenter realizes the import of the position he
is taking can be seen in his statement:

"For religion to supply one motive [the motive of co-operation which he is advocating], and the economic world another which stands in direct and irreconcilable contradiction to it, is to breed a conflict whose first result is psychological distress, whose ultimate effect is the ruin of both the individual and organized society" (p. 11).

The two positions are irreconcilable, and it is tremendously embarrassing from his viewpoint because he believes that his co-operatives are the Christian order of brotherhood. The economic world where the profit motive is exercised does not stand in irreconcilable relationship to the teachings of true religion. The co-operatives are the brotherhood of man, according to Dr. Carpenter, and he wants this co-opera-tion to be established as a fundamental principle of society by the creation of co-operatives everywhere.

This system of co-operatives with its motive of love is to be set up so that men will have to co-operate whether they want to or not; if they will not work, then they will not eat. The co-operatives will not let them. This order compels men to "love" each other whether they want to or not—surely a strange conception of love! But this is what is involved all along the line—freedom versus force.

Capitalism, Dr. Carpenter declares, has had its day.

"Among its achievements has been democracy itself, with its conception of economic freedom. But that this freedom continue to exist, it must accept restraint and responsibility. And lest law be imposed upon the eco-nomic sphere from the outside, perhaps violently by the hand of a dictator, it must be self-imposed. There is but one alternative to external force and that is the spirit of co-operation" (pp. 34, 35).

If anyone wants incontrovertible evidence to prove that the Federal Council of the Churches of Christ in America, through its leadership, as the "voice of the churches," is asking us to change our entire free economy, in which private enterprise is the essential ingredient, for a controlled or self-imposed collectivism, we have it here. This is the kind of evidence that proves the thesis of this book.

How about the political application of these principles? Dr. Carpenter does not overlook this matter, and though our discussion has been from a purely religious standpoint, we should point out in the words of Dr. Carpenter himself how these men feel about the political setup in the United States.

"Historically, democracy is the counterpart, if not the twin, of capitalism" (p. 33).

In this relationship between democracy and capitalism the Government kept its hands off free enterprise. Dr. Carpenter calls it "a delightful marriage."

"The marriage lasted well over a hundred years. But the New Deal finally brought it to a finish. And the divorce brought capitalism and government face to face as antagonists. There is not the slightest chance of their ever arranging an amicable settlement" (p. 33).

Yes, democracy gave us capitalism; or, the principles of capitalism gave us democracy. Destroy capitalism and you destroy democracy. Destroy democracy and you will kill capitalism. Control the economy and you will have to control democracy. In a free economy you may have a free democracy. This is why the issues at stake are so far-reaching, and the rise of the tyrant is on the horizon.

Dr. Carpenter summons former Vice-President Wallace

to his side when he quotes from Mr. Wallace's book, "Whose Constitution?" as follows:

"Capitalism, while financially stronger today than ever before, is becoming more and more spiritually bankrupt. . . . In the economic world it is inevitable that more and more emphasis is going to be laid on the idea of co-operation as distinguished from free competition" (p. 63).

Then Dr. Carpenter reads from Congressman Jerry Voorhis' (California) book, "The Morale of Democracy":

"Co-operatives are inherently built on spiritual motives —they are the most Christian of business institutions. They cannot be selfish and succeed. Some men insist that we must have competition. Undoubtedly, that is true. But there can be competition for something other than profit, or than control of other men. There can be competition to accomplish something higher and better than getting money. Either this is true or else everything that has been taught us by the forces of Christianity is a lie. But it is not a lie" (p. 64).

It is perfectly clear that Congressman Voorhis has adopted the whole philosophy of the Federal Council's social program. He thinks that the co-operatives are Christian, and built on spiritual motives. Many high-minded men of sterling character have been and are being misled by these church leaders who say, "This is the way we should go."

The jacket covering Dr. Carpenter's book has, at its top, this statement of one of the secretaries of the Federal Council: "A testament of co-operation that is needed by all searchers for the way to peace.—Benson Y. Landis." The Federal Council cannot possibly shake off this tag.

G. BROMLEY OXNAM

In Bishop G. Bromley Oxnam we have perhaps the ablest leader for the radical philosophy of the Federal Council that American Protestantism has produced. He has recently become Bishop of the New York Area of the Methodist Church. He was chairman of the Methodist Crusade for Christ, and at Pittsburgh, November, 1944, he was elected president of the Federal Council of the Churches of Christ in America, an honor which he said was the greatest in his life. He is brilliant, winning, with a wealth of experience, and in our opinion the best possible leader for its cause that the Federal Council could have in this hour. He makes the communist idea sound really Christian.

"Preaching in a Revolutionary Age" is his most recent book (1944), and is the Lyman Beecher Lectures on Preaching delivered at Yale University Divinity School. His study, report, and analysis of the world situation as being revolutionary is accurate and stirring, but the burden of his lectures is an appeal to the young preachers, in the name of Christ, in the name of Christianity, by means of Christian terminology, to go forth and take their places on the side of the revolutionary forces that would give us a planned economy. His work and leadership offer the most subtle and the most dangerous possible approach and presentation of these matters to the American public. This book is one continuous appeal for the new order based upon these new principles of co-operation versus the competitive struggle, personality versus the profit motive. And he calls for "common-good planning," not only in the terms of our national life, but also on the whole international plane.

"There must be over-all planning in terms of the whole world. 'Impossible,' 'Too vast,' it is said. I think not. . . . The planning can be done" (p. 109).

"The planning suggested here, democratic, growing out of need, seeking the fullest freedom of the person consonant with the freedom of the people, has been discussed on a national basis. But it cannot rest here. Just as planning by the producer or the consumer will not do—it must be by all—planning by one nation will not do" (pp. 108, 109).

Dr. Oxnam maintains that the fundamental, organizing principles of our present social order—profit motive, competition, incentives for production, distribution, and consumption—are unjust. The comprehensive sweep of his whole conception and the burden resting upon the church to supply the motive or new spirit are given to us in two paragraphs in his chapter, "A Common Faith and a Common Purpose."

"When the preacher affirms, 'I believe in God the Father Almighty . . . and in Jesus Christ his only Son our Lord,' he must make that faith meaningful in terms of action. How can belief in Jesus Christ be related to the fact that workers no longer hold that the injustice they seek to remove is caused by the meanness of their employers, although there is always the human factor in worker and employer making for discord, but rather that it is a matter of a system whose organizing principles are unjust, whose fundamental elements—such as production, distribution, and consumption—are at war with each other and therefore result in inefficiency. Is there no way whereby the faith of Jesus can be related to the issue, and the question of justice and the measures necessary thereto be determined in the light of Jesus' scale of values?

"If government derives its just power from the consent of the governed—and it is seen that the people possess a political power expressed in numbers that is less than the economic power of a small part of the people expressed in money—how can change be made so that all power shall rest on the consent of the governed, economic power as well as political power? It is precisely here that the danger to democracy is most threatening. If the people seek to bring economic power under their control and to direct it to worthy social ends, there is danger that ownership, which sees the threat to power that does lie in democracy, will abandon democracy itself in order to retain the power that lies in ownership. Reformer and revolutionist alike will do well to realize that regeneration is a need equally as imperative as change, either of consent or coercion. It is a new spirit that is our greatest need. Can religion supply it?" (pp. 78, 79.)

From the first paragraph it is clear that Dr. Oxnam identifies the faith of Jesus Christ, and his declaration from the familiar Apostles' Creed, with the new meaningful terms of action that will cut the very foundation from under unjust organizing principles and provide for us the just. That he projects these matters into the entire economic sphere and asks for a controlled society is clearly stated in the next paragraph. It is the people who are to bring economic power "under their control." This is dictatorship, the control of the proletariat. Then he continues to "direct it to worthy social ends."

The young ministers at Yale heard Dr. Oxnam declare, "The young revolutionary conceives of himself as a channel through which a larger purpose flows" (p. 57). And he emphasizes:

"Preaching must convince men that the application of the Christian ethic will bring greater security to the minds and spirits of all men and will elicit creative contribution from the genius for the benefit of his fellows because it obeys the law that co-operation and not selfish competition is the law of progress" (p. 75).

It is as clear as it can possibly be made that the church is the instrument of this revolution. The terminology of the Christian faith is the terminology of the revolution. The church's ministers are the prophets of the revolution. The church's people are to be the people who will cry out against the oppression of capitalism and the injustices of the profit motive, the tyrannies of competition.

Dr. Oxnam is fully aware of the import of the position he is advocating, and he struggles throughout his book with the logical contradictions. At one place he discusses the matter of the survival of private enterprise in such a co-operative order. For instance, he says:

"The common faith must come to live in the practices that make for brotherhood; the co-operative spirit must supplant competitive struggle; the objective of social endeavor must shift from profit making to personality making—not that private enterprise needs to go but that the spirit that infuses it shall be altered and the objective it pursues shall be changed. Such a faith is not the ruling faith of our day, if faith be tested by works. It is hard to change faith. Men have a tendency to believe in the system from which they have benefited" (p. 74).

Yes, the changing of the faith means the changing of the whole system from one of freedom in which there is the profit motive, competition—and from our viewpoint the only possible field in which personality can be developed in full responsibility to God—to one of control. But Dr. Oxnam feels the weight of the clash between his new system and the private enterprise system. Why does he say, "not that private enterprise needs to go"? His own logic, his own conscience, seem to impress upon him that that is the consequence. And it is! Yet he wants to save the private enterprise system. He wants to save it by taking the spirit out of it, putting into it another spirit, and changing its object. You cannot take the spirit out of anything and have it live. When the spirit which makes for the private enterprise system is removed, the private enterprise system collapses and expires, no matter how long a collectivist pulmotor is kept over the patient.

But the preacher in the revolutionary age needs more than faith, Dr. Oxnam continues:

"If in this century the group is resolved to make the externals minister to the essentials; if as a group we are going to do for all what few in religious circles have sought in service to do for a few; if we are to move up from the fighting way of life, beyond the money-making way of life, into an order that may be called the personality-making way of life; if we realize that men who have been trained to compete for self-interest will not do in an order that demands co-operation in the interests of the common good; if the engineer, economist, and executive are to take the ethical ideals and enthrone them in concrete reality; if we are to work out some splendid snythesis whereby the creative initiative that flowed from American individualism is preserved and the benefits that lie in collective action appropriated; then it becomes obvious and imperative that the preacher who serves in a revolutionary age must possess a preparation and a devotion akin to the scholars and the saints who in similar ages have been at once militant and meek, faithful and triumphant" (pp. 132, 133).

Dr. Oxnam's belief that some "synthesis" can be worked out that will preserve the creative initiative of individualism and the benefits of collective action is the delusion of the hour. It cannot be done. The creative initiative of individualism is the profit motive, and this must be destroyed before collective action can be established. Besides, who wants the benefits of this controlled economy at the price of the "creative initiative" of the individual? Why, why cannot these men see these contradictions in their own writings?

Constantly it is the contrast between the personality-making way of life and the profit or money-making way of life that Dr. Oxnam holds up before us. In regard to rationing he says:

> "Rationing is not only a matter of retarding inflation; it is feeding on the basis of personality rather than effective demand. . . . We seek the good man in the good society. Good men are apt to fight a losing fight in a bad society. We must make the conditions under which they wage their warfare as favorable to goodness as is socially possible" (p. 99).

One of the strongest delusions that has come over the minds of these religious, social-control planners is that human personality will develop better in their controlled order than in a free order. It is the conflict of competition, the responsibility of decisions, and the burden of those decisions that mold and develop character, and enable men to rise from strength to strength. It is in the free society where men are struggling with the issues of life, under the immutable moral laws of God, that they arise to be approved by that law or they fall to be condemned by it, and it is in this struggle that there is honor or shame, merit or blame, success or failure. These are the ingredients that make character, stability, and personality.

Of course, Dr. Oxnam is against regimentation in any form, but he uses the idea of the general staff of an army even though he recognizes that it involves the idea of regimentation. The democracy decides to go to war. That is the great over-all decision. Then the general staff goes to work. So it will be in this society of economic justice.

"The decision on the great ends is democratic. Again, and within the over-all decision, the execution is carried out in the multiplied units down to the last worker; but within the units, again, the democratic principle is present, the voice of the worker heard when management announces method and policy to attain its goal within the over-all objective" (p. 107).

It is the execution of these ideas that involves the tyranny, the regimentation, and the destruction of the development of the individual's personality. He becomes a serf, a slave, to the great ends of the plan.

Where these issues come out in the boldest perspective is in Dr. Oxnam's straightforward, throughgoing attack upon the individualist.

"The individualist seldom sees that the logic of his position is that of anarchism. The anarchist—and I need not here, I trust, point out that violence is no part of the creed of the philosophical anarchist—insists that personality flourishes only when free. Thus all restraint must be removed. Limitation of freedom is limitation of personality. He calls for no government at all, no restraint of any kind. This pushes the matter, we say, to absurdity. Perhaps. But what of the doctrine that government is best which governs least? The stress upon limitation beclouds the possibilities that lie in creative service by the government to the individual" (p. 88).

In the light of this paragraph Dr. Oxnam would call us the "anarchist." We do insist—America proves it—that personality flourishes only when free. But notice how Dr. Oxnam, as all of his kind do, now jumps the traces of reason and attempts to represent us as calling for no government at all. It is always liberty under law we demand, not life under the tyranny of the majority or the social group or the dictator that we must have!

Dr. Oxnam goes on. He even says that Herbert Hoover was the exponent for this plastic individualism. He applies it, too, to the political realm. Then Dr. Oxnam breaks with the idea that the government that governs least is the best. Free markets are unjust. This, he says, leaves the arena free for the expression of brutal selfishness. He wants to preserve, if possible, the creative initiative that flows from American individualism, and also secure the benefits of collective action. But the emphasis is all against the profit motive, and the preacher must preach against these things as sin. He is to use the authority of the Law and the Prophets and the Gospel, as he now understands them, against the sin of the old competitive struggle as opposed to the righteousness of the new co-operative order of brotherhood.

It is in the concluding chapter, "The Revolutionary Christ," that Dr. Oxnam moves on to the level in which he actually says that the real revolutionary involved in this is Christ. It is Christ's ideals that must destroy the profit motive and the competitive order; it is the application of

the Golden Rule. Furthermore, it is only when men are
willing to deny themselves, empty themselves, as He did,
that they will be willing to give up the system of private
enterprise, profit making, and be content to live in an order
where they shall co-operate peacefully and happily in an
economy that shall be collectively determined and controlled.

Jesus Christ, His good name, is used to lead the Christian
church into this system of tyranny. What has happened?
How does Dr. Oxnam understand Jesus Christ, to present
Him in such a thoroughly contradictory way from that
which we have pointed out in our earlier chapters? The
answer to this question will have to wait until we come to a
later section where we deal with the historic Christian faith.
There we shall show the real basis for the religious divergence; two different christs are involved.

JAMES MYERS

James Myers has done more than perhaps any other single
individual connected with the Federal Council of the
Churches of Christ in America to advance the social and
radical philosophy of the Council. He is the industrial secretary of the Federal Council, and it is his contacts and activity that have tied in the Federal Council program so directly
with the labor movement, and particularly the radical elements in the labor movement in the United States.

"Labor and Co-ops" is the title of a pamphlet by James
Myers. The second edition, which we have, was published
in October, 1943. Its subtitle is "The Value of Consumer
Cooperation to Organized Workers." We purchased it from
the literature table of the Federal Council in Pittsburgh in
November, 1944.

One of the effective ways to undermine a society based

upon the profit motive is to arouse in people, wherever possible, hostility against their neighbors who have made a profit. The field of labor is the most fertile ground in which to sow these seeds of hatred against the capitalist. You can never solve labor and capital relationships, in a free economy by convincing labor that the profit motive is wrong, for labor's hatred of the capitalist will only increase. The belief among religious leaders that the profit motive is inherently wrong finds its expression, in a myriad of ways, in the attack upon the capitalistic system. They must first tear down the capitalistic system before they can put up their controlled economy system.

Mr. Myers' booklet is an attack upon the system of private enterprise in a very subtle and clever appeal to labor to establish the consumer and similar co-operatives. He begins by rejoicing with labor's victory in securing collective bargaining; but he goes on to say that even collective bargaining is not enough. In this pamphlet we have an excellent illustration of the way in which the Federal Council leadership is leading the labor movement out beyond the legitimate bounds to which it can go within a free enterprise system. Collective bargaining is possible in a free enterprise system; but these other forms of collective activity that Mr. Myers now offers to the labor unions will utterly destroy the free system.

The most vicious aspect of this appeal is that Mr. Myers appeals to the profit motive as the reason for the establishing of the co-operative enterprise. When labor has made its gain through co-operative bargaining, then the prices go up and their gain is nil. "The cost of living robs your pay-envelope of the gains you have made through collective bargaining." So "collective action becomes absolutely necessary." Therefore, he declares, it is "common sense to organize your purchasing power." The laborer, therefore, will have more profit for himself, as the difference between his pay envelope and what he has to pay for materials—food, etc.,—will be larger. In other words, it is the profit motive with which Mr. Myers baits labor in order to destroy the profit system!

As he explains the consumer co-operative, Mr. Myers declares:

"It is highly important to understand clearly the true principles of a bona fide consumer cooperative for two reasons. First, many business enterprises now-a-days are *called* 'cooperatives' which do not meet the tests of a true consumer cooperative. They are often forms of profit enterprise for the benefit of private owners. All that glitters with the *word* 'cooperative' is not gold. Second, when a group sincerely desires to conduct a bona fide cooperative, they will want to know the exact principles of organization and operation which have now been tried out for nearly a hundred years and found to be sound and practical. Many failures have resulted when new groups started a cooperative without first studying and then strictly living up to these principles" (pp. 5, 6).

Here we have set before us the collectivistic attack upon private enterprise. Some of these co-operatives, he says, are misleading and deceptive because they are forms of profit enterprise for the benefit of private owners. What he is here attacking is the system of economy that has made America everything that she is. Then he takes pains to point out the different principles between what he calls producer co-operatives and instances where farmers co-operate simply to market their products. These may help the farmers get higher prices for their products, but it does not involve the principle of genuine co-operation without profit. This type of marketing co-operative is subject, he says, to the evils of profit business, including the temptation of such a group to exploit the market for its private gain like any other competitive profit-seeking company.

On the other hand, the consumer co-operative is owned by no individual. It is owned by the entire group. The first principle, he tells us, is that of brotherhood. Here we have a use of the term "brotherhood" as it is being employed constantly today to mislead men and actually to make them feel that what they are led to embrace is the Christian principle.

The second principle is that of economic democracy, and when our Federal Council leaders talk to us about an economic democracy, this is what they mean. Mr. Myers says:

"The second principle is that of 'economic democracy.' Each member has one vote—and only one vote—no matter how many shares of stock he may own. This is like our political democracy in which each citizen has one vote. It is like a labor union in which each member has one vote. It is, however, entirely different from the ordinary business corporation in which a stockholder is entitled to one vote for each share of stock he owns! A corporation thus acknowledges as most important the amount of *money* a person owns. A cooperative, on the other hand, holds the *human person* as the most important value and exalts him by giving him equal voting power regardless of the amount of his wealth. *A corporation in its very structure exalts the dollar. A cooperative exalts the person.* Is it not interesting to note how a mere clause in a constitution or a set of by-laws can express the basic principle of democracy which emphasizes the supreme value of the common man?" (pp. 7, 8.)

The third principle is what is called a balanced economy, and this does indeed have far-reaching results because it limits the individual return and destroys initiative, thrift, and risk which are essential ingredients of the free enterprise system.

The last principle is that of "business for service" and not for profit. In this system we have an attempt to put "personality" above profit, service above money, in a way that destroys the very nature of money itself. Money is an expression of an individual's labor, energy, and work. It is here declared that it is wrong to use that money to get gain. The laborer is exhorted to establish his co-operative so that he will save money, and, when he has been convinced of the entire idea, he is convinced that these principles require him to undertake to change the whole social order of America. This is the way the labor movement is being changed from a constructive and integral part of a free society to a revolutionary force to destroy our free society.

After discussing the growth of the co-operative idea in various sections of the world, Mr. Myers turns to the situation in the United States, and says:

"The cooperative movement in the United States has not yet grown to the proportions which it has reached in many countries. Perhaps our American idea—held until the depression hit us—that 'anyone can get on in America' and that 'prosperity is just around the corner' has made us less interested in making savings in our cost of living.

"To be quite frank, the slow growth of cooperatives in our industrial areas has been due also to the lack of sufficiently active support from the American labor movement" (p. 17).

"It is indeed encouraging that organized labor is now

showing an increasingly active interest. The current labor press carries news of the cooperative movement. Editorials in magazines printed by Railroad Brotherhoods heartily endorse the movement. The A. F. of L. and the C. I. O. and international and local unions have passed resolutions of approval and support, and have voted to set up special committees on cooperatives" (pp. 18, 20).

We then have a section dealing with the "Cooperative Credit" movement, organized, on a similar basis, as the consumer co-operative.

After setting these various plans before the laboring men, Mr. Myers is very plain in his appeal to the laborer to go on and on. The door is open; the path is now clear to do many radical things.

"They don't realize that they could go on up the path to *consumer-owned industry,*" Mr. Myers points out. "If they only knew it, they are already on their way! Organized labor does not need to make that mistake with its credit unions. Begin with credit unions *but don't stop* until you own and operate large cooperative enterprises in many fields. You can supply cooperatively your many needs in groceries, gasoline, insurance, medical service and many other necessities of life—even burial cooperatives which greatly reduce 'the high cost of dying'!" (p. 27.)

Just in passing, let me say, the Federal Council in its information service for Saturday, November 4, 1944, launched a full-fledged attack upon the undertakers of the United States for the high cost of funerals, and ended with a full and favorable presentation of the co-operative undertakers association or Co-operative Burial Association.

In such a plan as we have just mentioned in regard to

groceries, gasoline, insurance, medical service, and funerals, private enterprise ceases to exist. No one has suggested the idea of a co-operative dying association. No, the germ that killed the individual in his real place in life and society is co-operatively injected into men when they embrace this co-operative philosophy. The scheme kills and destroys liberty and human dignity.

The conclusion of the entire pamphlet again holds before us the title, "Industrial and Economic Democracy." Mr. Myers tells us:

> "Consumer Cooperation restores to the common people the *opportunity*—so largely lost even in this country—to practice the distinctly American virtues of self-reliance, self-respect, self-determination—to develop in this country *economic democracy* as well as industrial and political democracy" (p. 41).

Nothing could be more deceptive or untrue. The consumer co-operative does not establish self-reliance. It is group reliance. It is not self-respect. It is group respect. It is not self-determination. It is group determination. To lead the American laboring man to think that it is self-reliance, self-respect, and self-determination that is being established by his embracing the co-operative idea is a manifestly deceptive, as well as an exceedingly subtle, method to employ. America *can* lose her freedom!

It is so easy to point out the fallacies and flaws in this setup. When the co-operative idea exists in small units scattered across the country and these units make their profits in the competitive field with business enterprise, they do not seem to be dangerous; but when the idea that gives them reality finds expression in a larger sphere, when the co-operative reaches the stage where it either becomes a monopoly or controls the determination of prices and of goods, then the disastrous effects of both a cruel monopoly and a controlled society are wrapped together in one package. One way to establish communism in our country is to press this idea on and on, and go on down the road, as Mr. Myers has done in his appeal to laborers. Nobody owns the business. They all own the store.

The best answer to this, however, can be taken right out of their own advice. One thing upon which they have insisted in the establishment of the co-operatives is the open shop. Everybody must join. It must not be closed. Many laboring men are fighting for a closed shop in their bargaining contracts, but it must be an open shop for the co-operatives. That is the way the co-operative grows and gains and gets members. But Mr. Myers quotes the advice of Jacob Baker, chairman of the President's Commission to Study Co-operatives Abroad, and later president of the United Federal Workers of America, as saying:

> "It is very unwise to attempt to limit cooperative activity to a union group. For one thing, it doesn't work, and for another, it is a bad idea because it sets a fence around union members at a place where no fence should exist" (p. 39).

But when the co-operative idea embraces the entire social unit, we shall have the union group with the closed shop; and Jacob Baker is right. It does not work. These co-operatives fail. Mr. Myers gives one stern warning concerning management, and it is in this warning that we see the real weakness of the collectivistic idea. To summarize it, the essential qualities that make for the management of private enterprise are absolutely necessary to operate the co-operative. When the group selects a manager, it must do so not because the manager is a good seller or one of high standing in the union, but because he is a good businessman.

In dealing with the union inside the co-operatives, Mr. Myers says that the best practices of union relations, which have been worked out in many privately owned industries over a long period of years, should be studied by the directors of the co-operatives. It takes these virtues of private enterprise to make any business go, even if it is a collectivistic business, and if these virtues are not there, then the business suffers. When the individual is put in a place where these virtues are not naturally brought into play as they are in the "competitive market," the profit motive system of free economy, your whole setup is inherently wrong and headed for trouble.

Mr. Myers warns against bringing in relatives and kinfolk. It is so easy, we are told, in a system where profit does not count and where it is a matter of service—it is so easy in a system where gain is not to be considered, but where it is a matter of love and co-operation—to let down on the strict matters of accounting and thrift, the guarding of waste; and the temptation to steal increases.

The far greater damage of this co-operative idea, however, as being advocated by the Federal Council, is that these ideas are being engendered in the minds of laboring men as the ideas of the Christian faith, and though they may not find their expression in the changing of our way of life through the co-operative itself, they will find their expression in other ways when they become more generally current, in ways that can change society in a much speedier fashion.

E. STANLEY JONES

A popular propagator of the ideas that are so definitely Marxian, and the man with the widest possible opportunity to present them in the United States, is Dr. E. Stanley Jones. We heard Dr. E. G. Homrighausen of Princeton Seminary, chairman of the Federal Council's Department on Evangelism, say that the Federal Council had found Dr. Jones to be the most popular of all their speakers. Hundreds throng to hear him. He was the outstanding speaker of the Federal Council in their preaching missions; people all over the country idolize him. He is considered, by some, to be a prophet, and he himself actually says that he received the vision of his world federal union of churches from the Lord.

Dr. Jones' constant thesis is his near-communistic "kingdom of God." It runs through his various writings. But this kingdom of God is the establishment of a society that is to replace capitalism, go beyond communism, and give us the ordered, controlled, and "free society" in which, according to Dr. Jones, man was made by God.

"The Christ of the American Road," written in 1944, is Dr. Jones' latest book, and is heralded by many as his greatest. The burden of this book is the same as in his others. There must be a new social order. The conflicts of the present day can never be resolved until this kingdom of God is actually established by us. We are to bring in the kingdom. From the old theological standpoint it is postmillennialism ending in communism.

Dr. Jones takes the deeper things of the Scripture and deals with them in such a perverted and yet in such a subtle manner that he easily misleads Christian people. His appeal in this book is not to the laboring man, as was the case in Mr. Myers' work, but to the Christian—the Christian mind, the Christian conscience, the Christian young person. In the application of the idea of collectivism, he employs the phraseology of Scripture and the whole appeal of the Christian faith, in the most attractive possible way. When men hear him preach, they think he is preaching the Christian faith. In very fact, he is offering them Marxist ideas, sugar-coated with Christian terms. He takes texts that apply to the church and uses them to apply to the kingdom of God as a social order. This is where his twist and deadly error arise.

Dr. Jones gives us his theme text of this fresh approach to the idea of his "kingdom of God" society:

"The Christian faith must be a reconciling, unity-bringing power. How? By compromise? By appeasement? No, by reconciling men on a higher level by getting each to change. This verse, describing this possibility of recon-ciliation, became luminous to me at the beginning of the war, and has remained luminous, my chief guiding star amid the encircling gloom: 'To make peace by the crea-tion of a new Man in himself out of both parties.' (Eph. 2:15—Moffatt.) The clash was between Jew and Gentile —each feeling he had a right to rule, the Jew because of a divine destiny and call, and the Roman Gentile because he had the imperialistic might. A man stepped into that situa-tion who was eminently fitted to reconcile both, for he was a Jew and yet a Roman citizen. But more, he was a Christian, and as a Christian he got hold of a principle of reconciliation—a new principle. He saw that if Jew con-quered Gentile there would be no peace; there would be only planned revenge; and if the Gentile conquered the Jew it would be the same. Conquest would be followed by revenge, and the whole thing would seesaw down through the warring years" (p. 118).

This text, of course, actually means that by the new crea-tion, by the new birth, Jew and Gentile were brought to-gether in the bonds of the church of the Lord Jesus Christ, and so were reconciled to God and made one in Christ. It was not a question of the Jews conquering the Christians or the Christians conquering the Jews or the Romans conquering the Jews. The Jews remained Jews and the Romans remained Romans, but, by the power of the new birth in their hearts, they were able to love each other!

Yet in taking this text, falsely understood, as a method of reconciliation, Dr. Jones goes on now to apply it to the conflict between individualism and collectivism. He does this in his chapter, "The Application of the Principle of the New Man Out of Both Parties":

> "Both individualism and collectivism are half-truths, and life founded on either one of them alone will ultimately go to pieces. Individualism forgets that life is social, and collectivism forgets that life is individual and personal. I therefore reject both of them as ways of life. And yet I would retain the truth in each. How?
>
> "The answer is to be found in the doctrine of the new man out of both parties. The world is in a conflict—a global conflict over two great rival life-patterns, individualism and collectivism. In the kickback from individualism three great movements arose as intended correctives: Fascism, Nazism, and Communism. All three of these are intended correctives of individualism, and all three are intended to be organized around the same instinct, and all three are intended to go in the same direction" (pp. 126, 127).

He then discusses the nature of each one and says that all three "are going in the direction of the enlargement of the area of co-operation—the application of the herd instinct." He declares that the reason there is clash in war between these ideologies is that "they all stop short in their co-operative endeavor."

"Then what is the remedy? If we cannot go to Fascism, Nazism, or Communism, then where do we go? Back to individualism? We cannot. For individualism is outgrown; it is too small a basis for life. For life is seen to be social as well as individual. Then where do we go? The Christian has the answer in his doctrine of the new man out of both parties. . . . Suppose you could get them both to change—that would mean the renunciation of the error in each—and get them both to come to a third position beyond each, gathering up the truth in each, so that out of the two would emerge the new man; would that make peace? It would, for neither one would conquer the other, but something beyond each would conquer both" (p. 128).

This, Dr. Jones insists, is the kingdom of God.

"The Kingdom of God gathers up into itself the truth in individualism and the truth in collectivism and yet goes beyond each. The end is not a compromise, or an amalgam of both, but is a new product—a new man out of both parties" (pp. 128, 129).

Here, in this strange application, Dr. Jones destroys the whole basis of the individual. The freedom of individualism cannot be reconciled with the tyranny of collectivism. The two cannot go together to something that is beyond, because there is no beyond to freedom! You have reached the ultimate when you have freedom. To move on to something that is beyond is to leave your freedom and embrace something else. Dr. Jones uses a very subtle and brilliant twist to make people think they can go to something beyond individualism or the free enterprise system in which individualism alone can exist.

Dr. Jones is very hard on individualism.

"This last summer I listened to two rare and beautiful souls, with well-trained minds, say before study classes the following: 'The individual is of paramount importance,' and, 'The individual is an end in himself.' Both of those statements are at complete variance with the Christian faith" (pp. 124, 125).

The doctrine of individualism is working havoc in American life, Dr. Jones thinks; furthermore, he uses illustrations of extreme license.

Dr. Jones seeks to advance the above statement in contrast to the text, "Seek ye first the kingdom of God." He says it is not a question of seeking first the individual. The Christian faith, as we have seen in our earlier section, emphasizes the paramount importance of the individual. It is his decision, his choice, that determines the issues of life for him. The individual is an end in himself in that sense.

But one of the most astonishing revelations, so far as Dr. Jones' plan is concerned, is that, as he follows it out with sheer logic, without realizing it he gives the complete breakdown of his system. He says, for instance:

"In the Kingdom of God collectivism is fulfilled, for the Kingdom of God is a divine *society*. It is a social order, and that order is completely totalitarian; it demands the allegiance of everything and everybody in the whole of life. While collectivism is fulfilled in the Kingdom, so also is individualism. For the individual in seeking first the Kingdom of God finds that everything is added to him— including himself. As he loses his life in this ultimate allegiance, he finds it again. It comes back to him, released and free" (p. 129).

This is the society that man—Dr. Jones and our generation —must establish! This divine society, to be brought in by man, is to be completely totalitarian! If it be completely totalitarian, it cannot be free. It cannot possibly be free if it be a controlled society. Dr. Jones is right. Totalitarianism demands the allegiance of everything and everybody in the whole of life. That is the very nature of totalitarianism. This society, according to Dr. Jones, is what Jesus Christ held before us in His talk of the kingdom!

The individualism that Dr. Jones feels is fulfilled in this collectivism is an individualism of what the "kingdom" thinks is good for the individual and not what the individual himself thinks is good for himself. So far as losing his life in this ultimate allegiance is concerned, if he is willing to surrender his own ideas, his own freedom, his own moral welfare in this ultimate allegiance, then totalitarianism gives it back to him again, released and free within the bounds of totalitarianism. It is the freedom of the slave, if that can mean anything. What a debased, what a debauched idea of freedom! What a travesty of the kingdom of God! For Dr. Jones to take that great text, "Seek ye first the kingdom of God," to mean, "Seek ye first this collectivistic social order," and to say that "all these things shall be added unto you," meaning that this social order will take care of your security and comforts and give you liberty, is the mammoth perversion of the Scripture in this twentieth century, for it is a lie that takes us down the road that leads to tyranny. Does Dr. Jones really think that we can establish this kingdom of God, this total collectivism on the earth, and call it a divine society? There is no doubt about it so far as his mind and zeal are concerned.

But he gives us some additional light on the tyrannies of his kingdom:

"The Kingdom of God is the complete totalitarianism

which, when obeyed, gives complete freedom in the total life. Since we wouldn't choose this Kingdom through intelligent choice, the rise of the pseudo-totalitarianisms was inevitable. They rose as a reaction against individualism. God did not inspire their rise, but he has used them as a hammer of judgment upon our selfish individualism" (p. 130).

The Biblical truth, however, is just the opposite. The tyranny of Europe arose, and individualism is under attack today, even by Dr. Jones, because, and only because, nations and men have departed from the conception of man and of freedom given by God in the Bible to the human race. The Bible alone gives us individualism! Take away the knowledge of the Bible and the God revealed there, and collectivism arises.

Dr. Jones then goes on to tell us that it has been the insistence upon this selfish individualism that has led to war and ruin. We must repent of this sin of individualism and, as a prodigal, come home to God, willing to accept the totalitarian kingdom. The war, Dr. Jones tells us, will have destroyed the worst forms of collectivism.

"Then two great powers will be left: America embodying individualism and Russia embodying collectivism. America represents individualism at its best, and Russia represents collectivism at its best. Two great systems will face each other. In mortal combat as to which will master the world? Yes, unless they both decide to change and make a new man out of both parties—a world co-operative man. In that reconciliation on a higher level each will contribute something to the other. For each by itself is incomplete" (pp. 130, 131).

How can one possibly incorporate a free society with a

collectivistic society and have anything left but a collectivistic society? That "reconciliation on a higher level," the thing that America will receive from Russia, will be totalitarianism! What we are to give to Russia will certainly not be individualism, for, if she received such, her collectivism would cease!

This is one of the outstanding churchmen of the day speaking, telling us that we must take Russia's collectivism and give Russia our individualism! Why not each keep what he has, rather than trade?

Dr. Jones continues: "A combination of individualism and collectivism will give us what we need" (p. 131). You could no more combine individualism and collectivism than you could join light and darkness. The two ideas are mutually exclusive; they are two different worlds. In one, man is free and the State serves the end of man; in the other, man serves the end of the group, and he is no longer free.

But Dr. Jones says:

> "We will probably give to Russia the first commandment, 'Thou shalt love the Lord thy God,' and they will give to us the second, 'Thou shalt love thy neighbor as thyself.' Both will be richer. For while they represent individualism and collectivism at their best, their best is not good enough" (p. 131).

Think of ungodly, atheistic Russia giving to the world the second commandment, "Thou shalt love thy neighbor as thyself"! The Russian system knows nothing of what the Bible means by loving one's neighbor. No man can even begin to appreciate or love his neighbor until first he loves God, and that love of God can come only as he knows Jesus Christ as his personal Saviour and Lord. No man can possibly love his neighbor when what is called "love" is forced from him by the iron grasp of the tyrant's hand in which he himself is held. It is only in a free society that love for one's neighbor can express itself in any reality and with any ethical value. There are no ethical values in a totalitarian state.

This principle of the new man Dr. Jones applies to American life, and he says that labor and industry must submit to the rule that he has discovered in the Scriptures. He declares:

"But if capital tries to conquer labor and suppress it, then there will be no peace; there will be planned revenges, strikes, slowdowns, obstruction. I am also persuaded that if labor tries to conquer capital, again there will be no peace. But if you both change and come to the new man in industry—the co-operative man—that will make peace. For in that new man the legitimate rights of capital and the legitimate rights of labor will be gathered up and embodied. Neither one will conquer the other, but both will be conquered by something beyond themselves—co-operation. The new man will be the co-operative man—co-operating in production, in management, and in the division of profits and losses. Without the sharing of profits and losses the rest would be hollow and meaningless. It must be a thoroughgoing co-operation so that the peace may be thoroughgoing and not merely a patched-up truce. If you want the Christian Church to help produce that new man, then we are at your disposal. But you cannot ask us to play the role of giving the old sick man of selfish interests a periodic shot of kindly advice in the arm so that he may feel a little better—a little more virtuous. We are out to produce the new man" (pp. 135, 136).

The new man of co-operation is the new man of communism, for this thoroughgoing co-operation in production and management, profit and loss, and so forth, is the collective ownership principle. It is nothing more than the means of production being put into the hands of all for the good of all.

The same twist, the same perversion of thought that we saw in the application of this so-called new-man principle to the international realm, Dr. Jones applies here to the national realm for the extinction not of the labor side of the conflict but of the capitalistic side, and both parties are swallowed by the labor side of the conflict. The idea of going on to the so-called "new man" is a subtle way of getting the capitalistic side to capitulate to the collectivism of radical labor. This is all it is! It is not the laboring man who is swallowed up, but the capitalist—private enterprise.

But, Dr. Jones emphasizes here that the Christian church is "out to produce the new man." Here you have the attack on the great thesis of private enterprise, individual liberty, and initiative, an attack by this so-called Christian religion, this modern church, and it is being done by the church, in the name of Jesus Christ. What better evidence could one possibly produce to prove the thesis of this book?

According to Dr. Jones, free enterprise is "a dog-eat-dog economy," while controlled economy is "a brother-help-brother economy."

"American industrialism can choose one of these three attitudes: (1) 'I am my brother's boss,' (2) 'I am my brother's keeper,' or (3) 'I am my brother's brother.' The first represents autocracy, the second charity, and the third brotherhood. We have outgrown the first; autocracy in Hitler and autocracy in industry are two of a kind, and both must go. Nor will charity do. It is easy to be charitable; it is essential to be just. Only the third, 'I am my brother's brother,' is essentially right. And only on that basis will an economy be stable" (p. 141).

In the broad field of Christian conduct all three of these positions may be represented in a Christian's relationship to man. (1) If he employs men, he is his brother's boss for a few hours a day, as he directs his labor—private enterprise under the right of contract. (2) As a man, living in society, he must in benevolence help to take care of the poor and needy; charity is an essential ingredient of private enterprise. (3) "I am my brother's brother" is true of one Christian to another Christian only. But Dr. Jones' "brother" interpretation in society is the communistic idea of the equality that prevails under the totalitarian system. It can be that only when he contrasts it with the two previously mentioned attitudes. It is the controlled economy, he says, that alone will be stable. In many and varied ways Dr. Jones constantly comes back to this same thesis.

In his closing chapter, "What of the Future?" he speaks about the love of success as being characteristic of America. We want to succeed—that is the profit motive, the desire of our civilization. Dr. Jones says:

"Let our success be harnessed to the collective good—we succeed only as we help others to succeed. In helping others to succeed, then, it redounds in real success in us; we grow tall in helping others to their feet. The drive of the success motive must be detached from individual self-centeredness and attached to the public good—to the making of a society where the success of one is the success of all and the success of all is the success of the one. Then success will be redeemed. Now success is not redemptive; it is destructive. . . . A dog-eat-dog economy must be replaced by a society of mutual aid. Success must be success only as it helps oneself and others to succeed" (pp. 241, 242).

By such clever, yet clear, twists as these Dr. Jones tries to redirect our American life, or, as he says, "replace" it by a society of mutual aid—his collectivistic notion of the kingdom of God. Surely this is revolutionary. He calls it "The Christ of the American Road," and challenges us to cast off our un-American and unchristian hesitation and walk boldly the American road with Christ. He tells us, in his climax, that we have "a Cause—the Cause of causes, the Kingdom of God," and he would have us crusade to establish this kingdom of God in America by the collectivistic social order that he has outlined. Dr. Jones is a leader of the revolution!

In this chapter we have given the testimony of leaders directly connected with the Federal Council of the Churches of Christ in America. We have secured the very best possible witnesses—the head of the Department on Co-operation, the president of the Council, the industrial secretary of the Council, and the man who is considered their ablest missionary and most effective evangelist. Evangelism has a new meaning and content to these men. To lead the revolution for the new social order is evangelism to them. This explains why they always speak on the same theme—the new social order—controlled economy versus individualism. This is the program of the Federal Council as it is presented to us through the passion, the mission, and the message of these men. They are regarded as the leaders in American Protestantism. In the name and upon the authority of Jesus Christ they are offering to us a carefully worked-out attack upon our system of free economy and private enterprise as a fulfillment of the kingdom of God upon earth. We have endeavored to be fair to them, but their words speak for themselves; their ideas are in bold contrast to the verities of Scripture. This presents to America a problem of the greatest possible importance. What if these ideas should prevail? Where would America, free America, be? What is being done to meet and to challenge this vigorous campaign?

CHAPTER 7

INTERNATIONAL COLLECTIVISM

AN IDEA is not confined to a nation or a people. It roams the world; or, a better figure today is that it flies with the speed of radio. Especially is this true of the ideas of churchmen. Their ideas live first in the "international" sphere. It is the world they are out to conquer, for the kingdom of God as a social order cannot be the kingdom until it is universal.

The emphasis of the Federal Council of the Churches of Christ in America upon its social, radical program is becoming more pronounced, and the Council is seeking in every possible way to extend it. Dr. Samuel McCrea Cavert, general secretary of the Federal Council, gave the keynote address at the Pittsburgh Biennial, November 28, 1944, on "Major Trends and Problems on the Federal Council's Horizon." Speaking of this very matter of the social ideals of the churches, Dr. Cavert declared:

"Ever since its formation this Council has sounded the note of *Christian social responsibility*. At its first meeting in 1908 it set forth 'The Social Ideals of the Churches' and it has never ceased to be a center for a united witness to what the mind of Christ requires in the life of society. The years of postwar reconstruction will call for greater, not less, emphasis along this line" (p. 8).

One major field of Federal Council activity is seen in its support and testimony of the World Council of Churches, now in process of formation and which, when completed, will be the voice of the evangelical churches, even though

the Eastern Orthodox churches, un-Protestant and unevan-
gelical groups, are already in it. Concerning this matter Dr.
Cavert declared in his Pittsburgh address:

"We in the Federal Council rejoice in our opportunity
of helping to further the World Council. We see in it the
extension of the spirit and principles which have ani-
mated the Federal Council for thirty-six years" (p. 10).

The emphasis, of course, on this global World Council is
in what is called the ecumenical movement—world Christian
unity. We are not discussing that aspect of the Federal
Council's work in this treatise, as we have dealt with it fully
in our book, "Twentieth Century Reformation." But we
are interested here in the use the Federal Council is making of its relationship to the World Council, and the World
Council's testimony itself in the promotion of these radical,
revolutionary ideas that attack the private enterprise system
and the profit motive.

Bishop Oxnam's book, which we considered in our previous chapter, calls for one-world planning on a world
scheme. His ideals and idea demand it. E. Stanley Jones
definitely projects his whole kingdom of God as universal,
covering the entire world, his collectivistic ideas involving
every nation. It may seem like a dream to us, but it is not
to them, and the present world crisis is the golden opportunity of the Federal Council leaders to steal the show. Russia's place in the United Nations, and the general desire on
the part of every people to co-operate with other nations in
securing the peace, have given to the Federal Council the
greatest door in its history through which to walk as the
leader of international co-operation. But this international
co-operation means a great deal more than the ordinary

American envisions by the words. Words are so deceptive! It is convenient just now to have them so.

America wants to co-operate to keep the peace and maintain a free world, certainly not to establish a world collectivistic order. The essential, underlying conflict at the San Francisco Conference was just this. Russia represents collectivism; America, freedom; and the serious difficulties of world order are all found in the ideological conflict between the two. The Federal Council's idea is on the side of Russia in this conflict, not on the side of free America. Its program means an international, collectivistic order.

Consequently, in the last three years and more, since the United States entered the war, the Federal Council's big program has been its Commission on a Just and Durable Peace, and the Six Pillars of Peace that it has held up before the nation. These Six Pillars of Peace are so radical, at least the last five of them are, that when John Foster Dulles, chairman at that time of the Federal Council's Commission on a Just and Durable Peace, reported to the Pittsburgh Biennial concerning the relationship between the Dumbarton Oaks plan for international collaboration and the Six Pillars of Peace, he could say only that so far as the Six Pillars were concerned Dumbarton Oaks fulfilled simply the one. It gave the political framework for continuing collaboration. Mr. Dulles later resigned his chairmanship of the Federal Council's Commission in order to attend the San Francisco Conference in April, 1945, as a counselor for the United States delegation.

At Princeton, N. J., in July, 1943, the Federal Council, through its Commission on a Just and Durable Peace, held an international round table of Christian leaders which issued a Christian message on world order. In the light of all that we have seen in the Federal Council's nationalistic propaganda in the United States, the statements in this message are not only understandable but also indicative of the future developments that the Federal Council leaders expect as the result of their social ideals propaganda. The report said:

> "Any planning for world order calls for special consideration of the relationship to such world order of the ideals and practices of the U.S.S.R. The Russian revolution is one of the great facts of our time, and its consequences will be central for many years.
>
> "In form, and to a large extent in practice, the Russian revolution has been anti-religious and materialistic. If that continues to be the case, we cannot disguise our concern. That would prevent a world community of spirit which is an indispensable foundation of world order.
>
> "But we need not assume that this will be the case. . . .
>
> "We believe that as Christian people demonstrate that they can achieve such beneficent social ends as are sought by the Russian revolution—and much more besides—many differences between us will tend to disappear. We need not now act on the assumption that those differences will persist to create a permanent barrier to world order."

What could possibly be meant by the statement, "Many differences between us will tend to disappear"? It is simply this: If we change over to a controlled, economic democracy for our social order, then Russia will be very happy to cooperate. Russia, of course, will be pleased to join a world order when we can show her that we are seeking the ends obtained by the Russian revolution. That the Federal Council through its program wants these social ends that exist in Russia cannot possibly be doubted when it is the international field in which these ideas can be put into effect without

the full scrutiny or the possible understanding of their impli-
cation by the people of the United States. It will be so easy
to pack these radical ideas in the coach marked "Co-operation," which the American people desire. And it is in the
economic council of the world security organization that
these ideas may especially be seen; also in the sphere of
international finance.

Let us look at the Six Pillars of Peace for a moment. These
Pillars will have a continuing importance in the years ahead,
for they state the goals toward which the religious leaders
desire to direct the international security organization. The
Pillars are as follows:

"I. The peace must provide the political framework
for a continuing collaboration of the United Nations and,
in due course, of neutral and enemy nations.

"II. The peace must make provision for bringing within
the scope of international agreement those economic and
financial acts of national governments which have widespread international repercussions.

"III. The peace must make provision for an organization to adapt the treaty structure of the world to changing
underlying conditions.

"IV. The peace must proclaim the goal of autonomy for
subject peoples, and it must establish international organization to assure and to supervise the realization of that
end.

"V. The peace must establish procedures for controlling
military establishments everywhere.

"VI. The peace must establish in principle, and seek to
achieve in practice, the right of individuals everywhere
to religious and intellectual liberty."

These Six Pillars, we are told in an introductory remark,

"serve to force the initial and vital decision on the direction in which this nation will move. They force that decision in relation to six major areas within which the factual interdependence of the world has become such as to require political mechanism for cooperative action."

With this idea, as intimated here, comes the entire system of economic planning and collectivism that the Federal Council is advocating on the home front. If a "just and durable peace" is conditioned on these propositions being realized, then a "just and durable peace" is impossible in the world, for these goals cannot and will not be realized in this world of sin and brutality in the heart of man.

Let us look at these propositions. It will be much more effective if we begin at the last and work back.

"VI. The peace must establish in principle, and seek to achieve in practice, the right of individuals everywhere to religious and intellectual liberty."

It is the very freedom recommended here that the system of planned economy and social control destroys. Russia, in which true religious freedom and intellectual liberty no longer exist, is one of the main parties to the peace. Russia is coming out of the present war in a most powerful position, and to demand of Russia, as a condition of peace, that she give intellectual and religious liberty to her people, in the sense in which we understand it in a free economy in the United States, is simply absurd. If Russia were weak and helpless, she might consider such a request, but with her strength she is in a position to refuse to make such a "surrender"—for such she would consider it—to the "weak" democratic ideals.

To use these words of freedom as a basis of union or unity

in a world security organization, with Russia understanding one thing by them and Great Britain and the United States understanding another, would be double talk and a vicious form of deception and dishonesty. The world is in a very serious state of affairs, and America must not, ostrich fashion, hide her head in the sand, or be duped with a false peace and a deceptive calm.

The news from the Yalta Conference has not satisfied the world on these vital questions. In reference to the Atlantic Charter, the two liberties that were mentioned in the Crimea Conference declaration were freedom from want and freedom from fear. Russia is supposed to have these two freedoms, according to her ideology at least, and apparently, rather than embarrass Russia by putting in freedom of religion and freedom of speech as the first two liberties, Roosevelt and Churchill did not raise the question. Furthermore, we do not desire freedom from want and fear in the sense that Russia defines and exhibits it. Religious and intellectual liberty in the sense in which we know it would destroy Russian communism, and this is really the inherent reason why Russian communism, when it came to power, crushed the church and the Bible, and slaughtered Christians by the millions. We may as well red-pencil that Pillar now. The world structure, depending upon that Pillar, will never exist so long as Stalin remains Stalin. Russian ideology is the logical hindrance to world peace.

We could have peace if the world were totally "collectivistic." This is Dr. Carpenter's "peace through co-operation." We could have peace if the world were totally "free" in our American sense—a world association of free states. But it is the logically irreconcilable nature of the two ideologies, the different concepts of freedom, the conflicting nature of the two systems all along the line, that clash, and clash, and clash, and that inevitably, in time, cannot help but produce trouble. One system has one moral code; the other, another. For this reason the question, Can Russia be trusted? is so pertinent. May God help us! So long as this situation exists, and it will always exist unless Russia or America changes, both sides enter a world organization with their fingers crossed or with mental reservations, while the real factor behind the scenes is the power of the democracies versus the power of the collectivistic states.

"V. The peace must establish procedures for controlling military establishments everywhere."

This is a fine ideal, and everybody would like to see it accepted—but will Russia and the United States consent to have some international body control the size of their military establishments? We doubt it very seriously. Following the last war, treaty provisions controlling military establishments compelled Great Britain and the United States to scrap their navies, but at the same time opened the door for the speedy rearmament of Japan and Germany. One of the strange delusions of the Federal Council's peace program is that it does not realize that such things as spheres of influence and power politics are inevitable ingredients of our world. We can get rid of them only by a totalitarianism that rules the entire world, and this, of course, is where they, with their program, are trying to lead us.

At the present time the United States has its sphere of influence, and Russia and England have theirs, whether we like it or not. To attempt to destroy these spheres would be just as futile as to attempt to destroy the spheres of influence of the sun or the moon. Smaller nations in close proximity to these larger powers are going to determine their conduct by the influences that come from the larger groups. According to the Yalta pronouncement, the one thing that stands out is that Stalin has agreed that in the matter of voting in the international association setup the majority vote will prevail for questions relating to smaller countries, but if any questions of major importance involving sanctions against Soviet Russia are raised, then there must be unanimous decision. This means that the world conference has collapsed before it has started so far as a security for peace is concerned. This means that Stalin has decided to keep in his own power the control of his own military establishments and of his own house. So let us check off proposition Number V. If this stands, Stalin is, without dispute, the No. 1 man of the world.

"IV. The peace must proclaim the goal of autonomy for subject peoples, and it must establish international organization to assure and to supervise the realization of that end."

This platform appears more absurd in the light of the Yalta Conference and the decision that was made with regard to Poland. Stalin got his demand for a larger slice of land. The concessions that he made were that the Lublin Government would have to be dissolved and a new government established to include portions of all parties represented in Poland. But how about the subject Poles in the occupied territory that has been given to Russia? How about the autonomy for these subject people? Yes, we talk about the establishing of an international organization to supervise such an end while we are actually compelling a portion of the Polish people to become members of the Soviet Union. We may as well check off that proposition, too, before we proceed any farther. If these professed principles will not work to solve a present problem, neither will they hold in a future crisis.

"III. The peace must make provision for an organization to adapt the treaty structure of the world to changing underlying conditions."

Some international organization will adjust and determine the treaty provisions for the various countries and nations. This power which is, according to the American Constitution, now vested in the United States Senate, will have to be modified to have the Senate adjust these treaties according to the recommendation or action of the international organization. In the adjustment of such treaties, there are far-reaching consequences for the play of all kinds of political forces. Nations can be strengthened. Nations can be weakened. In the name of compromise, groups can be penalized. The partitioning of Poland at Yalta was done in the name of compromise.

Proposition II tells us that the international organization

"must make provision for bringing within the scope of international agreement those economic and financial acts of national governments which have widespread international repercussions."

Here we have international economic and financial control. The determining of the economic and financial structure on an international basis will, of course, determine it on a national basis for every country in the world, including the United States.

Here is planned economy on an international scale. This, of course, would appeal and undoubtedly does appeal to Russia. She could work very efficiently in an international organization along the lines of planned economy because she is the one who has had most of the experience in such planning. With the Federal Council's approval of her ideas, and with its molding of public opinion in the United States, as it is endeavoring to do through the works of such men as E. Stanley Jones and Dr. Oxnam, we could finally be led to accept some of the Russian ideas in regard to international planning, and the whole world would be delivered over to Russia. That is exactly where we are headed, just as straight as a die, if this grandiose scheme, this utopia of the Federal Council, is followed.

We have one Pillar left to support the framework of peace, according to the Federal Council:

"I. The peace must provide the political framework for a continuing collaboration of the United Nations and, in due course, of neutral and enemy nations."

This is a good Pillar, because in such a framework of collaboration there can be discussion, and it is our duty to live peaceably with people so far as is possible. In such a structure we can work together, and there will be an opportunity for the free play of power—political, economic, financial, and otherwise.

It is just as essential, on an international scale, that we have a free world, a free economy, an uncontrolled international economy, as it is that we have a free economy on a national scale for the development of a nation. In a free international economy, the same forces for the development of the individual are at play as in a free national economy. In such a free economy the United States has come to her place of power and influence. No forces have been able to hold her down. Her advantages, her privileges, her culture, her life have been possible because of the free world in which our nation has developed. We must keep it free.

The Federal Council has set before us a scheme as fanciful as "Alice in Wonderland," the carrying out of which would involve us all in a world of tyranny. But these are the Pillars of Peace, the political propositions that the Federal Council says underliȩ a "just and durable peace" that the United States ought now to accept for herself and begin forthwith to realize in co-operation with others.

In its second national study group in Cleveland, Ohio, the Federal Council gave to Dumbarton Oaks its unqualified approval but made a number of recommendations for its correction and improvement. These recommendations and suggestions are all in line with the last five Pillars of the Federal Council's Six Pillars of Peace. They are agitating, they are working, they are endeavoring to move all the forces they possibly can in support of this international organization that will control economy, finance, and armament. And then, in such a controlled and regimented society, the United States will have to sit in the place assigned to her from above.

The solution for all this is to demand a free world wherein the forces of enterprise can run free. Jesus Christ stated the principle in Mark 3:27, "No man can enter into a strong man's house, and spoil his goods, except he will first bind the strong man; and then he will spoil his house." In other words, if the United States wants to keep her house, she must be strong enough to keep it, or a stronger will come and take it from her. In the ultimate and final analysis, the only real language that Russia will understand, as she sees America putting her confidence in a world security organization to whose success and for whose continuing existence Russia alone has the key, will be not only the actual military strength but also the degree of preparedness and potential military power of the democracies.

America must remain armed. We cannot gloss over irreconcilable ideologies, no matter how earnestly we endeavor to get along with the Russians. We cannot permit ourselves again to lapse into a false sense of security such as that which gave Hitler the green light.

This is the Federal Council's peace program born of its collectivistic ideas. It is infinitely more dangerous than a rattlesnake. The effect of it all in our own national life will be to leave us helpless before Russia, more so even than we were before Germany and Japan when the Second World War began.

Leaders in the World Council of Churches, however, realize the importance of all this. Dr. W. A. Visser 't Hooft, in an article entitled, "Social and Political Forces of Tomorrow," discusses the situation in Europe. Dr. 't Hooft, with offices in Geneva, Switzerland, is the general secretary of the World Council of Churches (in process of formation). He starts his article by telling us of the "landslide in society." In it, he says, we can detect three factors: the bankruptcy and collapse of the bourgeoisie in many countries, the manifestation of the preponderant role of the workers in modern society, the new prestige of communism. The article, written as a report, nevertheless reflects, in a number of ways, the attitude of the writer himself. There is nothing in it to indicate that the system of free economy, or capitalism, should be fought for, or that society should "turn back" to it. In fact his whole vision is the other way. He says:

"Let us now try to define the ideologies, the forces, which will have the greatest influence in the world after the war. I can see three, which I shall call 'liberalism,' 'socialism,' and 'communism' " (p. 6).

They are, he says, the same international forces that penetrate almost everywhere. "We shall first of all consider them in isolation." Liberalism, he says, is the oldest of the ideas, but "it will not be the orthodox liberalism of earlier days." "Such a liberalism will accept the principle of planning, and a directed economy." This liberalism, he says, will take up a position against every attempt to limit economic liberty from the state or from the workers. But, he says,

"This liberalism lives today as it always does on a sort of rationalist idealism mixed with a great deal of hypocrisy, . . . which is of benefit to certain classes of the community" (p. 7).

"*Communism* is the youngest and the most vigorous of the three ideas. It wears the halo of success in one great country, and has not yet had the opportunity to compromise itself in the others" (p. 7).

He continues:

"So the communist party scarcely speaks now of class-warfare; in many countries it manifests an almost exaggerated patriotism; it makes advances to the Christians. The communist party in Holland says: 'We deny the existence of God. But we recognize the right of other people to propagate their convictions. If the Christians will apply their conception of love of their neighbor then the basis of collaboration exists' " (p. 7).

"Socialism," he says, "has ceased to be a class affair"; and "the feeling that the capitalist age is nearing its end is shared by men in all social groupings."

Dr. 't Hooft has this to say about the common denominator of the three systems:

"They all aim at conquering capitalist anarchy, not

only by means of a certain degree of reorganization and co-ordination of economic forces, but also by means of a radical social transformation, that is to say by making those who control the chief means of production clearly responsible to the community, and by making democracy effective in the economic sphere" (p. 8).

So he concludes that the present-day socialism "then sanctions a controlled and guided economy." How similar all this language is to that employed by Drs. Carpenter, Oxnam, Myers, and Jones!

This is the general secretary of the World Council of Churches speaking, and he sees no place whatever in the future forces of society for private enterprise in a free economy. This is the goal of the Federal Council's philosophy and program.

The words "international co-operation" should be defined for the United States. What do they mean? The word "co-operation," like the word "co-operative" is vague, and may mean many different degrees of working together. There is little doubt what the Federal Council means by the terms, yet, because the words are vague and undefined, it is profitable in advancing its ideas. We must not be deceived.

America has fought for freedom—not the Russian idea of freedom, but the American idea written in the Bill of Rights. Only in a free world can these freedoms live. So far as "ideologies" are concerned, the battle to preserve them will really be just beginning when World War II is ended. Unless we are put on our guard and go to work to meet the flood of propaganda now engulfing us, the ideas now being established in the deceptive and subtle use of words such as "brotherhood," "democracy," "co-operation," and even "liberty" are laying the foundation for the rise of the tyrant.

CHAPTER 8

UNITS OF THE REVOLUTION

LET us turn back again for a few minutes to the United States and consider the condition produced by the Federal Council propaganda as it affects the people. How about the individual denominations that make up the Federal Council? These are the churches to which the majority of American Christians belong. Twenty-five separate denominations, or national church bodies, make up the Federal Council. If these denominations did not belong to it, there would not be a Council. The strength of the Council depends upon the number of its denominations and the number of communicants in them.

In recent years the Federal Council has made a number of important gains of which it has been very proud. In 1938, the Protestant Episcopal Church united with the Council, and in 1942 the Council elected as its president the head of the Episcopal Church, Bishop Henry St. George Tucker. In 1941, the Presbyterian Church in the U.S., the Southern Presbyterian Church, went back into the Council, and they honored this denomination by electing one of its leaders to be vice-president in 1942. The Federal Council is stronger today than it has ever been.

The ideas that the Federal Council propagates and emphasizes, as we noticed in the chapters dealing with its social ideals and the views of its outstanding leaders, are not the views of an isolated group, or a little clique that has taken over the Federal Council and is running it. The Federal Council is the first to deny such a thought. It is responsible to the denominations that comprise it; it speaks for them. Therefore, what the Federal Council does is to express not only the united voice of these groups but also the views and position of the dominant groups within the Council. What we are saying is that the local churches, the individual denominations inside the Federal Council, are not merely implicated in this program of radicalism that we have considered, but they are the ones who have made the program possible. Their leaders, their assemblies, their conventions, their conferences have adopted resolutions dealing with the social issues in which these same radical ideas are dominant. In fact it was here that these ideas were first heard. We must not blame the Federal Council alone without placing the fullest responsibility upon the churches that have made the Council what it is. We would not be fair to our readers, nor would we be fair to the Federal Council, if we neglected to point out, by reference to evidence, the radical nature of some of these groups. We are thinking particularly of the Methodists, the Presbyterians, the Baptists, and the Congregational Christian groups. These are the leading forces of the Federal Council.

"Christian Unity in War-Time" is the title of a very attractive pamphlet issued by the Federal Council, a copy of which we secured in Pittsburgh in 1944. On page 5, the Council, after listing the names of the denominations that are members, declared:

"As the Council was brought into being by the Churches, so also is it wholly responsible to them. Organized on a strictly representative principle, it is governed by approximately 450 delegated representatives, all appointed directly by the constituent denominations. These representatives, in their biennial meetings, constitute a central board of interdenominational strategy, developing a common mind, planning united policies and providing for concerted action. In the interim, an executive committee, made up of 80 members, all of whom also are named directly by the cooperating Churches, meets bi-monthly for the supervision of all the Council's work."

My, how significantly the phrase "developing a common mind" stands out in this statement, for the "common mind," as developed and expressed, is this very social, radical program.

It is on the basis of this structure that the Federal Council legitimately makes the claim:

"The Federal Council is the official agency through which twenty-five national denominations, comprising 140,000 local congregations, with a total membership of more than 25,000,000 join in common tasks. By reason of its fundamental concern with Christian cooperation the Council holds a unique place in strengthening the spiritual foundations of our national life" (p. 3).

And to strengthen "the spiritual foundations of our national life," according to the program of the Council, is to change the entire basis of our social order. What better evidence of the subtle yet major attack being made upon our free enterprise system could possibly be produced?

The General Assembly of the Presbyterian Church in the U.S.A., the denomination to which the general secretary of the Federal Council belongs, issued a pronouncement in 1934 dealing with this matter of the profit motive and replacing it with other motives:

"We recommend that new motives besides those of money-making and self-interest be developed in order that we may develop an economic system more consistent with Christian ideals."

In this pronouncement the denomination itself put its General Assembly on record in a statement that cuts the very heart out of our whole economic system, the profit motive; and it goes on to say that other motives substituted for the money-making motive will "develop an economic system."

The second point, however, of this Presbyterian pronouncement, as recommended to the General Assembly by the Committee on Social and Industrial Relations of the Board of National Missions and approved by the Board of National Missions itself before presentation to the General Assembly and its adoption there, went even farther. It read:

"That competition as the major controlling principle of our economic life be re-examined, and an attempt made to secure rational planning in our economic life."

In this declaration of the church we see a planned economy as opposed to the free competitive order. Nothing could be plainer.

But the third provision in this pronouncement goes a step farther:

"That our natural resources and economic institutions be considered as existing for the public good and such plans for ownership and control be developed as will lead to the best use in the interests of all."

This is only another way of stating the principles set forth in the Russian Constitution. These resources and the economic institutions are not for the basis of private enterprise and free economy. They exist for the public good, for ownership and control in the interests of all.

Point 4 of this social pronouncement again projects this idea on the international scale:

> "That cooperative economic life be developed on an international scale both because of the need for peaceful international relations and for the fullest development of the world's resources."

Here is the philosophy behind the Federal Council's peace program, as we saw it in the last chapter. Here is the entire program of the international co-operative, or collectivistic economic life, which, in the terms of Dr. Oxnam and Dr. Carpenter, alone can give peace. In this thoroughgoing and far-reaching declaration adopted by the Presbyterians, one thing is sure; it is that this will change the present economic system and develop something else. But this new system in which the profit motive and the money-making idea will no longer be the motive and idea of enterprise will be "more consistent with Christian ideals."

In 1932, the same year the Federal Council adopted its Social Creed, the Presbyterian Church in the U.S.A., meeting in Denver, Colo., adopted a platform of social "Ideals and Objectives." The preamble to this Creed reads as follows:

> "In view of these obligations, the Presbyterian Church in the U.S.A. does now declare and stand for the following ideals and objectives:
> "1.   Practical application of acknowledged Christian principles to the acquisition and use of wealth; subordination of profit to the creative and cooperative spirit; observances of such social plans and control as are involved in the economic process which operates for the common good."

Here again we have the socialistic philosophy stated as it is constantly being restated and emphasized by the Federal Council. One of the recommendations immediately following these ideals is the following:

"That the Board of National Missions and the Board of Christian Education be directed to incorporate a study of social and industrial relations in the schools and colleges under their respective jurisdictions where not now done."

Likewise, the seminaries were requested to give definite attention to the preparation of the students to meet the responsibility that the social and industrial situation is now laying upon the ministry.

It is with this very thoroughness that the denominations inside the Federal Council have been carrying on their propaganda for the new collectivistic social order. How many Presbyterian businessmen know that this is what their church—the church they support—believes and declares to the present generation?

Year after year the General Assembly of the Presbyterian Church in the U.S.A. has reaffirmed its social pronouncements and has always given its social emphasis. In 1943, the Council, in a long report and action by its Social Education and Action Committee, presented the Six Pillars of Peace of the Federal Council, as we have considered them in a previous chapter, and declared:

"That General Assembly commend these Political Propositions as being in keeping with Christian principles essential to the establishment of world order under law in the interests of justice, liberty, and peace."

The Assembly also recommended that synods, presbyteries, local churches, and the agencies of the church support these six political propositions in Congressional or Senate action.

In one very penetrating paragraph the Assembly, in reference to an action it took the previous year, recognizes the change that is taking place, and we note especially their concord with the reappraisal that must be made of capitalism. It reads as follows:

"We concur in the view expressed in the following words of the last (1942) General Assembly: 'We are witnessing the death of one age and the birth of another and we must be prepared for far-reaching changes in the conventional framework of our lives and in the national and international order. As a result there will necessarily be a reappraisal of nationalism, of capitalism, and of all existing ecclesiasticisms. The Church is challenged to accept the inevitability of this change and to direct this reappraisal to the end that there may be established a new brotherhood more closely approximating the Kingdom of God.' Within our own nation this social transformation is being made by persuasion and under law; but the war is a sign of man's failure to make the same degree of social progress on a world-wide scale. We believe that a society which is on the march to a new ordering of its human relationships is to the Christian's opportunity, to further among men the Kingdom of God who makes all things new."

Immediately following the above quoted paragraph there is an additional sentence that gives us the existing contrast which the church recognizes:

"This vast penetrating and swiftly moving social change is apparent in the shift of emphasis from what we have called individualism, with its stress on the rights of the individual, to various forms of collective effort, with their emphasis on solidarity."

Yes, this is the conflict. Yes, and the principles on which the Presbyterian Church in the U.S.A. has based its program throw it on the side of the collectivistic emphasis and no longer on the side of individualism which alone can have in it democracy and private enterprise. The tragedy of one whole great denomination's going over completely to socialistic dogma is appalling, but the Federal Council could not possibly have its place of power and its voice in America today unless more than one church sustained this view.

The Northern Baptist Convention is one of the best known spokesmen for Baptists in the United States. It has gone over to what is called modernism in the church; and hundreds of Baptist churches, in order to be true to the Baptist faith, have withdrawn from the Convention. Among the Convention's prominent leaders are such men as Daniel A. Poling and Harry Emerson Fosdick. Rochester Divinity School and Crozer Theological Seminary are among its most radical institutions.

This church has gone over to the socialistic conception of society. The Northern Baptist Convention's Postwar Planning Commission, 152 Madison Avenue, New York 16, N. Y., has recently issued a pamphlet entitled, "Postwar Aims." We are told concerning this representation:

"This document, prepared by the Postwar Planning Commission of the Northern Baptist Convention, is an attempt to state in broad terms, the great objectives of the Christian enterprise.

"It is designed primarily for the Commission's own use as a norm by which to measure the work of all denominational agencies, and to discover what further steps each needs to take to meet its responsibilities and grasp its opportunities now and in the postwar world.

"It is also prepared with the further hope that it may be widely useful to our churches, to organizations in the churches, and to individuals, to clarify our immediate objectives, appraise our motives and our service, and to enlarge our vision and our goals. In particular, it may help pastors and churches to plan a full, rounded, and balanced program.

"Produced first for the Commission's own use, it is now issued to the denomination for whatever value it may have in making our ministry to this suffering world more helpful."

It is in Section 8, "To Apply the Laws of God to Economic Life," that we see championed and explained the very kernel of the Federal Council's anti-Biblical position. The fifth point under this section is:

"Furnish the dynamic for obtaining economic justice for all people. *a.* Proclaim with courage and conviction the basic and urgent necessity of attaining the yet un-realized goals of economic and political democracy in our national and international life. *b.* By emphasizing the values of human personality and the dignity and worth of all people, Christians must inspire social and economic pioneering for the common good."

Here we have the familiar phraseology of the Federal Council. Here we have the same collectivistic ideology pre-sented—"social and economic pioneering for the common good"; "economic . . . democracy in our national and inter-national life." These declarations involve the first two planks in the Federal Council's Social Creed.

That we are not misunderstanding this emphasis in the Northern Baptist Convention is clearly revealed in the pamphlet, "How Labor and the Church Can Work Together," dated March, 1945, and written by the Rev. James Myers, whom we have considered previously. This document bears the imprint of the Federal Council of the Churches of Christ in America and is "distributed by Council on Christian Social Progress of the Northern Baptist Convention, 152 Madison Avenue, New York 16, N. Y."

On page 2 of this pamphlet we are told:

"If, as a labor man or woman, you believe that 'the churches are neither thinking or doing anything about social justice'—just send to the following organizations for information about the social pronouncements and programs of their faith or denomination."

The first group mentioned is "Industrial Division, The Federal Council of the Churches of Christ in America, 297 Fourth Avenue, New York 10, N. Y."

We know what their social pronouncements are! We have considered in detail the core of their Social Creed. We give this information to indicate how perfectly the program of the church is synchronizing with the program of the Federal Council. The two are inseparably enmeshed.

In his introductory paragraph Mr. Myers has this to say about labor and the church:

"In fact, prophetic church leaders have seen in the labor movement a vital expression of democracy itself—a means through which the common people can attain the dignity and self respect and equality which is their due as children of God. Labor and the church share common ground in their basic objective of human welfare."

The leaders in the Northern Baptist Convention are not blind to what they are doing. They are fully aware of the radical nature of the program they are offering and of their endeavor to solicit the backing and support of the radical labor movements for their revolutionary propaganda. The pamphlets they publish are attractive. They come in the name of the church and for the "betterment of humanity." As a matter of fact, the introduction of the pamphlet, "Postwar Aims," seems to emphasize the place of the individual, to reaffirm the historic Baptist position. These radical ideas are being placed in the most attractive kind of vehicle. It is a much more unsuspected instrument than the Trojan horse. It is the "angel of light"!

The Northern Baptist Convention has gone all out in its support of the co-operatives which Mr. Myers discussed for us previously. At the meeting of the Convention in Atlantic City, May, 1944, it adopted certain resolutions on economic and industrial issues. One of them declares:

> "*Resolved,* that our government should foster a program of domestic reconstruction at the close of the war which would be committed to the following general purposes: . . . 11. The encouragement and protection of co-operatives."

These are the co-operatives which, Mr. James Myers tells us, will bring in the new economic age, the co-operatives which, according to Dr. Carpenter, destroy the whole system of free enterprise and the profit motive. The Northern Baptist Convention is carrying its share of the load in this battle for the changing of our social order. It is in the truest sense of the word a unit in the revolution.

The main emphasis of the Methodist Church during the war has been this program of the Federal Council for a new socialistic order. Under the leadership of Bishop Oxnam the Methodists launched a crusade for a new world order.

Such a name is harmless, and it sounds good. We do not want a world of war, and the longing of people everywhere is that this world shall be replaced by a better one. Almost everybody could be enlisted in such a crusade, regardless of who they are. But what is the nature of this new world order for which we are crusading? It is identically the same as we have seen emphasized by these church leaders.

The Methodist Church at its General Conference in Kansas City, May 5, 1944, adopted a social creed that was a re-emphasis of matters for which it has been standing for many years. Section 9 of that creed repeats the familiar phraseology that we have quoted a number of times before— "the practical application of the Christian principle of social well-being to the acquisition and use of wealth and the subordination of the profit motive to the creative and co-operative spirit." Will they ever stop attacking the profit motive? This is, word for word, Plank No. 1 of the Federal Council Social Creed!

The Methodist Church has been the most vigorous of all the denominations in this country in favor of the radical ideas that are so dominant in the Federal Council's platform. It is in one of their pronouncements in 1940 that the Methodist Church actually takes its phraseology from the Federal Council's platform of 1932:

"We stand for the principle of the acquisition of property by Christian processes, and believe in stressing the principle of stewardship in its use; in the practical application of the Christian principle of social well-being to the acquisition and use of wealth and the subordination of the profit motive to the creative and co-operative spirit."

The Methodist creed also emphasizes the concept of the universal Fatherhood of God which is the basis of all this false thinking concerning the economic brotherhood:

"We believe that God is Father of all peoples and races, Jesus Christ is his Son, that we and all men are brothers, and that man is of infinite worth as a child of God."

How wonderful that would be if it were true! But it is not. We are not brothers one of another, nor are we children of God until first we have been born again.

This Methodist crusade, however, has had the most powerful propaganda pushing it. A large brochure entitled "A Report by the Chairman," and filled with pictures of reports of actions and the outlining of the program of the crusade, was published April 5, 1944. The Six Pillars of Peace, which we analyzed in detail in our previous chapter, are the program for world order, and the emphasis is mainly upon the economic controls which must give us peace in the international world.

It is on page 4 that we see how closely the program is tied in with the Federal Council, and there is no question but that the Methodist Church really intends to be an effective unit in the struggle for a new social order based upon these unchristian concepts.

"The Federal Council of the Churches of Christ in America is rendering signal service through its Commission on the Bases of a Just and Durable Peace. But effective public opinion will be created by the great denominations that have the ability to reach the local parish. This Methodism must do."

Following the section in which the Six Pillars of Peace are separately dramatized, we have a section entitled, "Some

Lessons of the Crusade." The following is one of the sections:

". . . The Kingdom of God cannot be built upon foundations of economic injustice. The economic order must be rebased and remotivated. Unless the democratic peoples can retain their liberty and use it to establish equality, there is little hope of moving to fraternity. Therefore, the question of economic justice and racial brotherhoods at home is one of major importance. When the guns were silenced in 1918, the political war ended. But the economic war continued. No enduring peace can be built solely by setting up worldwide political agencies. The economic war that emerges from competitive struggle and the acceptance of self-interest as the driving force of economic endeavor will move out from the nation to the world, unless there be fundamental reordering in the economic field. This becomes a primary concern of the Church. The war of the nations must not be allowed to become a war of the classes."

When the economic order must be "rebased," and the economic field is fundamentally "reordered," have we not abandoned our free system?

Everything we saw in Dr. Oxnam's book and in Dr. Jones' "Christ of the American Road" is emphasized here again for us. Why do they talk about the war between the classes? It is the clash which is inevitable between a system of economy that is free, where the profit motive reigns, and a system of economy that is absolutely controlled by one class, the laborer, the proletariat.

Dr. Oxnam delivered an address before the conference of district superintendents of the Methodist Church in St. Louis, Mo., on September 26, 1944, and in this he told how effective this crusade has been:

"What did the Crusade for a New World Order do? You will remember its fundamental principle, namely, that the religious forces of the nation must become influential at the place decision is made, before it is made, so that our convictions may be regarded as creative and co-operative contributions. We did this by registering the opinion of the people called Methodists with our representatives. Mass meetings were held in 76 cities, with nearly 200,000 people in attendance. The literature of the church school was revised and millions of our youth studied the meaning of world order and were summoned to write their representatives. The devotional literature of the Church was similarly revised. Ministers preached upon this subject."

It is apparent that the whole church was ordered and used as a mighty unit in the promotion, not just of a new world order but of a particular kind of world order, one which involved an attack upon the profit motive.

Yes, we want to have peace, but we do not want to have a peace that will give us a world order that is regimented and controlled. When the church calls it the kingdom of God, when the church marshalls its forces to back such an idea in the name of religion, it has abandoned its function and its purpose as a church of the Lord Jesus Christ.

The Methodist Church, through its General Conference of 1944, issued a document entitled, "State of the Church." In a section dealing with economics we again see this same attack made upon the rights of private property and our free economic order:

"Where the rights of property conflict with the establishment of social justice or the general social welfare, those rights should be overridden, modified, or, if need be, abolished."

In addition, the church declared:

"We endorse the stand taken by the Delaware Conference (Federal Council of Churches): 'We believe that a new ordering of economic life is both imminent and imperative.' . . .

"We reaffirm the principle of the Commission to Study the Bases of a Just and Durable Peace of the Federal Council of Churches: 'The peace must make provision for bringing within the scope of international agreement those economic and financial acts of national governments which have widespread international repercussions.' "

Yes, it is the same international, economic regimentation that is a part of the whole collectivistic scheme for the ruling of the masses. The Federal Council leaders think it is Christianity. They think it is liberty. The Methodist Church has gone all out in support of this program, more so perhaps than any other of the Protestant denominations in the United States.

We have spoken of the Methodist, the Presbyterian, and the Baptist denominations, which are among the leaders and the most influential in the Federal Council. They are having a profound effect upon the other groups that are associated with them in the Federal Council.

"Is Everybody Out of Step but Us?" is the title of an article appearing in the *Presbyterian Outlook* for May 7, 1945, written by "The Editors." The *Presbyterian Outlook* is the voice of the liberals or the modernistic movement in the Southern Presbyterian Church. It is this group that is now leading that denomination. The emphasis of this article

is that the Southern Presbyterian Church has done nothing
to rally the people behind these new social ideals and to
lead the members of the denomination to understand the
kind of socially controlled economy that the world must
have in order to keep permanent peace. The article speaks
about the activities of the other units, so to speak, and chides
the Southern Presbyterian Church for failing to do its duty
in support of this great program of present-day Protestantism. We mention this to indicate the swing, the current, the
way in which the whole movement in the churches is going.
The article declares:

"The Evangelical and Reformed Church, with its Commission on Christian Social Action, has only recently
employed a full-time executive secretary for leadership in
this area. Its agency has the power to act in its own name
—not the church's name—as this is considered an essential
requirement for effective work. . . .

"Presbyterians, USA, through their nine-year-old Department of Social Education and Action, work under and
are financed by their Board of Christian Education with
an able and effective staff. . . .

"Another one of the best denominational agencies in
this field is that of the Congregational Christian Churches.
By its constitutional authority it conceives its responsibility as helping the churches of its communion in their
understanding and expression of the Christian's fulfil-
ment of what Christ spoke of as the second greatest
commandment. . . . Its magazine, *Social Action,* has a wide
influence.

"Northern Baptists have a three-year-old, independent
board, responsible to the general council and the annual
convention."

Of course, these social action groups promote some good things. They are against child labor and in favor of collective bargaining, etc. But all of these, as we have seen in the case of the Federal Council program, are nullified and vitiated by the thoroughgoing, revolutionary demands of their new social order in which the profit motive is replaced and the competitive struggle is at an end, and we have one totalitarian unit.

We could go on and quote from actions and literature of other denominations, but this is sufficient. The very fact that these denominations are in the Federal Council should be adequate to show their endorsement and approval of the Federal Council's social program, since that is the main emphasis of the Council, according to its own statement of purpose. The church leaders in these units are not unaware of these matters. They are heartily in sympathy with them, and are endeavoring to use their denominational strength in every possible way to advance their radical ideas. But they must be careful; they must not go too fast or too far beyond the people. That explains why we find these ideas interwoven as a part of a picture that does not look radical when an unsuspecting Christian picks up a pronouncement or reads a pamphlet that is handed to him with the kind words of his pastor.

Every denomination of the Federal Council is a part of this radical program. Each is in a very definite sense a unit of the revolution. It is not necessary to quote resolutions from every one of them. There are some which have not gone to the extreme, but they are in the fight for the new social order. Their strength, their presence, their good name, and their people are being used for the revolution. If these denominations were not in accord with the social program of the Federal Council with its attack upon the profit motive, they could very easily withdraw. The issue is serious enough to make any group withdraw, for it involves the changing of our entire American way of life and the infusing of a new idea.

CHAPTER 9

THE MARK OF THE BEAST

WHERE is all this attack upon the profit motive and the destruction of private enterprise leading us? Where are we going? Does the Bible give us any light on these questions? It most assuredly does. What we actually have here is not just two different economic systems, but two different religions,—one, the historic Christian faith based on the Scripture, which we shall discuss in its fuller aspect in our closing section, and the other, which is not Christianity at all. What it amounts to is that the Marxian philosophy has been adopted, and is offered to us in the name of Christianity. This means that the Marxist ideas and the implications of the Marxist philosophy are being ground into the phrases and expressions formerly used by the Christian religion. The forms of the Christian faith are being made the vehicle for the presentation of the communistic ideology. This is the same strategy as that used in taking our beloved American terminology—democracy, freedom, liberty, etc.—and grinding into it the Marxian ideas.

The point where these two different religions clash, so far as this discussion is concerned, is on the profit motive. To the Federal Council the profit motive is wrong and must be replaced; but the exercise of the profit motive involves the individual, and it means, therefore, that the individual is guilty of sin when he indulges in the profit motive. This is the principle that we previously saw denounced. This is the sin that Dr. Oxnam wants his young prophets of the revolution to rebuke with great vigor throughout the length

and breadth of the land. These two religions have entirely
different concepts of sin. These two religions have entirely
different concepts of the individual. These two religions
have entirely different concepts of society, of the moral law,
of the church, of the future of man. Most of all, they have
entirely different concepts of God. One has a God, the true
and living God, and the other has not. What it calls God
is in reality itself—the State, the Society. We shall see this
later.

As we have seen, the Bible recognizes that the profit motive is valid, but it condemns those who would gain profit
unlawfully by stealing or exploitation. It condemns those
who use in wrong ways the profit that they make legitimately.
God will judge them! We too must condemn them! But the
Federal Council men ignore this distinction and condemn
the profit motive, per se. Thus it is that a people and a
society are called to repent of sin when they are not guilty
of sin; they are asked, in the name of the church, to substitute
an entirely different order of society which will keep them
from their "sin."

One reason the Bible is so insistent upon a free economic
order is that only in such an order can a man's sin, real sin
in the true sense of the word, be kept from affecting the
whole of society, and each man bear the fullest possible
penalty for his own iniquity. In the planned co-operative
order that the Federal Council offers to us, the real sin in
the heart of man will work havoc with society in a multiplicity of directions where our present free society does not
suffer. Self-reliance, independence, and those other virtues
that are born because of the responsibility of the individual
for himself are left upon a siding to deteriorate while the
train of society goes on down the road to a fuller expression
of slothfulness, laziness, cheating, stealing, manifestations of

"black markets," and all other forms of the evading of control.

America's rationing system during the Second World War has revealed the sinfulness of the heart of man, and has brought into the open the cheating and lying that are there. In some realms the Government has actually had to retrace its steps, because, in order to enforce its rules, it would have had to invade the private homes and private lives of people. In order to preserve such a controlled society as the Federal Council advocates, the use of force becomes increasingly indispensable.

We have said that in the new social order there is an erroneous view of the individual. Yes, in this new order the individual "sins" when he exercises the profit motive; moreover, it is this same individual who, the Federal Council leaders are telling us, has great dignity and who is endowed with certain prerogatives that we must and will preserve in a co-operative society. Therefore, they tell us, we will remove his sin of using the profit motive! On the other hand, the Bible tells us that, at the present time, man has no dignity. He lost it all when our first parents fell into sin. Man in his present condition is depraved—totally, utterly depraved. "There is none righteous, no, not one" (Rom. 3:10). Man in the fullest possible sense is a beast. This is why a collectivistic society, controlled by man, is beastly. Man is worse than a beast, infinitely worse. There is no animal in existence that acts as man does today. Furthermore, it is this individual who will wreck any planned society unless he is put into a strait jacket. This is exactly what the planned society has to do with him in order to keep this society functioning and progressing! But this is tyranny; this is regimentation. It does not leave the individual free, but instead it gives the State or the group power over him.

Dr. Harry F. Ward, professor emeritus of Christian ethics of Union Theological Seminary, in the latter part of 1944 wrote "The Soviet Spirit." Dr. Ward has been a moving figure in Federal Council circles for years. In the chapter entitled "What's Ours Is Mine," he has this to say:

> "When the legal essence of private property—exclusive control—is abolished, there is nothing left for the possessive appetite to feed on. Even social ownership becomes a misleading term; it is not ownership at all in the old sense. It simmers down in fact to joint use and management and perhaps had better be called what it really is —social control" (p. 44).

In other words, when we have taken away man's opportunity for private property and profit, we have eliminated one of the great spheres of sin.

Dr. Ward, in his book, is advocating, with all his might and main, the adoption of the socialist idea as Russia practices it. In fact, he serves a good purpose, so far as our cause is concerned, because he identifies for us, in the most unmistakable manner, the use that is being made of these various words by Federal Council leaders. That they mean the same thing and refer to the same system that Russia has is proved beyond a doubt. For instance, he declares:

> "The essential difference between capitalist and socialist motivation is summarized in the proposal to organize production for use instead of profit, or, in the language of ethics, to substitute the will to serve for the will to gain. . . . They are generally classified under two opposing heads—self interest and the common good. Capitalism makes the common good depend upon self interest. Socialism changes the order and makes self interest depend upon the common good" (p. 16).

Here we have in the Federal Council propaganda the typical Russian philosophy; but from our viewpoint capitalism makes the "common good" depend upon the individual's liberty. Socialism changes the order and makes the individual's freedom depend upon the "common good."

But notice Dr. Ward's use of the popular slogans of the day. In them is dynamite to wreck America. "Will to serve" versus "will to gain," "self interest" versus "common good," "production for use" versus production for "profit"—here is the present battle ground of private enterprise versus controlled economy; and the American people by the thousands are being taken in by this talk while they sing of freedom and while their boys die on the battlefields of the world.

Before we go on, we ought to say a word about this socialized individual. The individual in a socialized society becomes an entirely different type of person from the one in a free society. Dr. Ward gives us an illustration of this:

"Recently I had the privilege of guiding and listening to an evening's discussion between some of the Soviet students now studying here and a selected group of American students. The differences that came out were even more illuminating than the likenesses. The Soviet group had difficulty in understanding what the Americans meant by the phrase 'social conscience.' This was partly because they had no knowledge of, and hence no responsibility for, unprivileged classes. The nearest they could come to that feeling of obligation was in relation to some of the backward nationalities now in the Soviet Union. But since equality of development is a constitutional guarantee and a rapid achievement, their situation is entirely different" (p. 145).

In this kind of society there will be no need for the application of the Book of Proverbs with its commands to look after those who are in need. Yes, we shall be able to get along without the Bible. In fact, we shall have to be without it, for its teachings demand the overthrow of the collectivistic society in order that man may serve his Maker.

A young man recently was honorably discharged from the United States Army and came home. His mother told us that he was having a difficult time adjusting himself because in the Army everything was planned for him, and now he has to go back to making his own decisions. The regimented man in the United States Army gives a little illustration of where regimentation and social control leave us—helpless, minus individualism!

The "common good" is an innocent-sounding term, but it is filled with all the tyranny of State control. When you say that the individual exists in society for the "common good," you have adopted the totalitarian philosophy, per se. From that point on, you are living in a totalitarian ideology and world. The individual is not an end in himself; his end is the contribution he can make to the good of the group. This is nothing more than the nazi national socialistic idea: that man exists for the good of the State. From the individual standpoint and the standpoint of the Scriptures, however, the greatest good a man can do, so far as the State is concerned, is to maintain his own freedom and liberty.

The use of the word "brotherhood" to include everyone is so subtle! We are told that, in the interests of brotherhood and the broad interests of humanity, we must be willing to relinquish our individual society, in which the profit motive operates, replacing it with the world of brotherhood. Such an idea of brotherhood, of course, is not found anywhere in the Bible. All men are not brothers. All are sinners and under the curse and wrath of God because of their transgressions. It is the brotherhood of the redeemed of which the Bible speaks—the church, the family of God. This is an elect, a called-out body, which actually becomes the salt of the earth. What we ought to be hearing is the phrase "good neighbor" instead of "brotherhood." We are neighbors one to another, according to the Bible.

When the socially determined "common good," however, becomes the end of society, anything that will interfere with that plan, disturb or disrupt it, is the enemy of society. The dissenter is guilty of sabotage, yea, of sin. He who would dare oppose or upset the "common good," as determined by the particular staff of planners that the group has established, would be condemned, and it is on these bases that the bloody purges in such systems are justified as moral. They are a violation of the moral law of which we hear so much today—brotherhood; we are all brothers. The system of economy that is planned, into which the individual must be fitted, has a moral code of its own, created out of the exigencies of the single-mindedness of the plan. When the so-called "common good," as decided by the group, becomes the end of the individual, then the Biblical teaching that the end of man is "to glorify God, and to enjoy him" must be discarded. Both ideas cannot be the "end of man."

Let us move a step forward and go a little more deeply into the heart of the real error of the planned order. The individual does not exist for himself—no, neither does he exist for society. He exists for God, and God has first priority on the individual, the totality of his life; anything that places the individual in such a circumstance that he must recognize the "common good" as the "end of man" in society actually usurps the position that God alone can occupy. When the individual exists for God, that individual is responsible to God. It is only in a free society where the individual is free to regulate the basic things of his life—his economy—that he can render to God an account of the gain and use of his possessions. It is these particular things that God Himself has so specifically regulated in the Ten Commandments. When the "common good" society with its own morals takes possession of a man, the Ten Commandments must be replaced. This has happened in Russia. They will inevitably be discarded in any such planned or co-operatively controlled society. This is why Russian policy is called "realistic," and none can predict the ethics of Russian action.

The "common good," however, from our viewpoint, is fulfilled in the greatest possible way when men in obedience to their God, their Creator, their Redeemer, obey the Ten Commandments. They give us the free social order, the right of property, and the responsibility of the individual not to what men may establish as the "common good," not to the State, but to God. No State can render to God an account for the individual. No collectivistic co-operative can render to God an account for the sinner. The attempt to do so destroys the individual; this is the reason personality is not developed in the co-operative order. How deceptive and vain are such slogans of Federal Council leaders as "We want personality, not profit"!

When the "common good," or the planned society, becomes the end to which the individual's whole life must be ordered and bent, the powers that are directing this "common good" must control the mind and the thinking of men to receive their support and co-operation for such "common good." This involves the control of all the avenues of propaganda, just as is done in Russia. Men will rebel, the plan will fail, there will be dissension and discord, and men will have to be put to death for sabotage. To have a planned society, it is necessary to control the elements that maintain the "common good," the most important element of which is the mind which controls the free actions of men. This mind must be controlled and to control it, education must be controlled, the home must be controlled, religion must be controlled, freedom of speech must be abridged, freedom of the press must be abridged, freedom of assembly must be abridged. The control of the mind of man for the maintenance of the plan is not economic democracy; it is not social justice. It is tyranny, blind tyranny, the darkest, blackest tyranny that the human race has ever seen.

However, in this progress, there is another advance that is inevitable and inescapable. When society takes the place of God in the life of the individual, it deposes God. Not only does it remove God, but also it enthrones itself in place of God; then it turns brutally and bitterly against God for even laying claim upon the life of the individual, and the society becomes anti-God, militantly atheistic. Who is to have the individual—God or the State? God claims him and orders freedom for him to serve the Lord. The State claims him and orders its plan to use him for its "common good."

There is the closest possible relation between the communistic, social control of the economic processes and Russian atheism. Atheism will produce a collectivized individual, and the collectivistic social order ends in atheism because it attempts to take the place of God in the lives of men. Such a controlled society binds man and carries him away. It steals him from God. When a wrong view of the individual is taken, the end is a wrong view of God, because God made the individual for Himself. When a wrong view of sin is taken and that pronounced to be sin that God has not called sin, the end is an entirely different moral code, which God did not give us, but which came from some other source.

The clashing ideas of private enterprise and a socially controlled society are irreconcilable. They are a focal point for the meeting of two entirely different religions—one in which the living God may reign in the heart and life and be free to receive the worship and the praise of the individual, and the other which has to turn against the living God in order to control the individual.

It ought to be clear now to everyone that in such a controlled society the church of Jesus Christ, the true church, will have to be gagged and bound. When the church turns to fight the "common good" group, to tell it that it has no right to steal the individual as it is doing, the "common good" group, which has the police powers, turns to crush and destroy the church. Thus it has been in every single State where the collectivistic idea has been embraced—Russia, Japan, Germany. Or, on the other hand, the church that does exist is a church that has become subservient and is willing to compromise with the commission it has received from Jesus Christ. Such a church is unworthy of the name.

The tyrannies of this collectivistic idea break out at different points even in the writings of the Federal Council men. For instance, we are told that in this planned, socially controlled society those who will not work shall not eat. In a free society, when a man will not work, he has to beg or suffer hunger. But in a controlled society, if he will not work he cannot beg, because nobody but the group has anything to give him. The group, through its power, enforces economic sanction and refuses to permit him to eat because he does not agree with their plan or thinks things should be done in some other way. The so-called conscientious objector cannot exist in such a society. If he did, the plan would collapse.

At this very hour American mothers and fathers are grieving for the loss of their boys and girls who have laid down their lives to free people throughout the world from just such tyranny. It is freedom, the love of freedom, which is bred into the hearts of our American boys, that has led them to go out and fight for freedom for themselves and others.

When these ideas of a planned and socially controlled society are presented to us, and it is pointed out that they involve a restriction upon liberty, we should be done with them. All the comfort, convenience, power, and security that may be offered to us in such a planned society are as nothing compared to the loss of liberty and freedom to serve God. But the ideas that involve tyranny and tragedy are offered to us in the name of the church which is supposed to defend freedom. The Bible has a name for it. It is apostasy, a falling away.

The Federal Council and its leaders have fallen away from the teaching of the Bible, and instead of bread it offers a stone by the name of strawberry shortcake. If the Christian people of America will wake up and assert themselves on this great issue, we can save our free land, if the Lord wills.

Surely the world is being prepared for the rise of the beast. When a nation of freedom-loving people, in the name of "freedom" and "democracy," is being taught by the church that the profit motive is sinful and individualism dead, the highway is being paved for the speedy rise of the terrible tyrant. When the "germ idea" of collectivism is planted in broad daylight in the garden of free men, it may, as it takes root, easily choke to death the tender plants of freedom. When men cry for security more than for liberty, then liberty is gone. The real security, and the only security worthy of the name, is liberty itself. Benjamin Franklin once said, "Those who would give up essential liberty to purchase a little temporary safety deserve neither liberty nor safety."

In the closing chapters of the Word of God we see the picture of a "beast coming up out of the earth." He is the dictator, and "he causeth all . . . to receive a mark in their right hand, or in their foreheads: and that no man might buy or sell, save he that had the mark, or the name of the beast, or the number of his name." Here is economic control, totalitarianism—the mark of the beast!

We call these last five chapters "The Modern Church," for such it is. We have endeavored to set forth, on the basis of evidence, that the Federal Council of the Churches of Christ in America, the voice of the modern church, is offering a radical idea that would utterly destroy private enterprise and free economy in the United States. We have examined the official actions of the Federal Council, the writings of its outstanding leaders, its projected world program, and some of the declarations of the churches that comprise the Council itself. We have followed logically the "idea" offered for the new social order, and have seen it in the light of God's commands for the individual.

Thus far, therefore, it is clear that the modern church is certainly not presenting to us the same message as that presented by the Word of God. Parts I and II of our study tell different stories. The Word of God teaches the profit motive; the modern church condemns it to be sinful. The Word of God teaches "individualism"; the modern church assails it as "chaos" and "selfishness." The Word of God reveals that private enterprise is the legitimate and lawful order for free men; the modern church would substitute a socially controlled economy into which all must fit. The modern church is in mortal combat with the position of the Bible. One says one thing; the other, another. To which shall we listen? Which shall we follow?

One other thing, however, is clear—as clear and bright as the noonday sun. In view of what we have seen, the circumstances that we now face in America are the gravest in the history of the nation.

But there are other questions, the answer to which may help us. How long has the church been giving us this message so different from that of the Bible? Did not our present social order of free economy come from the Bible? Why has someone not told us about these things before? What is being done to remedy the situation? What can we ourselves do now? These and other questions we shall answer in the third and last section of our study.

Part III

THE HISTORIC CHRISTIAN CHURCH

CHAPTER 10

THE CREEDS OF CHRISTENDOM

WHAT has happened? What has happened to the church? Surely the church has not stood in its testimony through the years for this planned social economy and this fulsome attack upon the profit motive as we have observed it in previous chapters. What has happened to Christian leaders that they are now advocating a program set in such bold relief against the commands and teachings of the Bible? What has the historic Christian church taught and believed in regard to these matters? These questions now naturally and logically press in upon us.

The historic Christian church has always stood by the Bible. The great creeds of Christendom, which summarize the teachings that men have always believed, support heartily and unanimously the principle of private enterprise, the validity of the profit motive, and the indestructible place of the individual in society. As a matter of fact, it is the Bible that gave us the individualism that produced capitalism and democracy. The historic Christian church gave us that system of free enterprise in our Western civilization. "If the Son therefore shall make you free, ye shall be free indeed" (John 8:36). "And ye shall know the truth, and the truth shall make you free" (v. 32). It is within the realm of being "free indeed" that the truths of the Scriptures as they apply to the individual demand democracy, freedom of conscience, freedom of religion, freedom of expression—press, radio, speech.

Though the modern church as represented through the

Federal Council is not on our side, there is a great measure of comfort in reading the creeds and being able to believe that we at least are in the train of our fathers when we lift our voice in behalf of these precious things. Others may depart from them, but we must remain true.

If the creeds of the church, as we are now going to point out, support the principles that we have outlined in the first section of this book, then it means that the creeds and the Bible are on the side of private enterprise, and the modern church is on the opposing side. This places the present-day modern church, as represented by the Federal Council, in a most unenviable position. In view of all that is involved as the consequence of its attack upon the profit motive, we can render no greater service to the cause of Christ and the liberty of America than to place the modern church before the X-ray of God's Word and the fluoroscope of the ancient creeds.

The Thirty-nine Articles of the Church of England, also the creed of the Episcopal Church in the United States, embody one article that clearly repudiates the whole communistic idea and supports the Biblical position of the profit motive and private enterprise. Article XXXVIII in the Latin edition of 1563, the English edition of 1571, and the American revision of 1801 reads the same. There has been no change. It declares:

"Of Christian Men's Goods, which are not common.
"The Riches and Goods of Christians are not common, as touching the right, title, and possession of the same; as certain Anabaptists do falsely boast. Notwithstanding, every man ought, of such things as he possesseth, liberally to give alms to the poor, according to his ability."

This creed of the Episcopal Church says that the individual's right to property is a definite and not a relative matter. In the light of this confession the idea of the consumer-co-operative, where the people hold things in common and the whole group owns everything, is repugnant to the historic creed. The entire emphasis of the Christian faith upon the individual's responsibility to gain by the profit motive, by such things as he possesses, and according to his ability, is in order that he may be able to help the poor.

The Methodist Articles of Religion of 1784, known as the Twenty-five Articles of Religion, drawn up by John Wesley for the American Methodists, constituted an abridgment of the Thirty-nine Articles of the Church of England. However, Article 38 became Article 24 with only one slight change. "As certain Anabaptists do falsely boast" was changed to read "as some do falsely boast." Yet, strange as it may appear, it is the bishop of the Methodist denomination today, Bishop Oxnam, also president of the Federal Council, whose social philosophy denies all this, and whose recent volume, "Preaching in a Revolutionary Age," repudiates it, calling for a reconsideration of the right and title of property. No better evidence of the change that has come over the Methodist Church could possibly be had than this.

If private enterprise and the profit motive are valid, as the Scriptures say they are, then any other system—such as communism, or the holding of goods in common—is wrong and sinful. The modern church says it is sinful to have a society built on the profit motive. The historic church says it is sinful to have a society built on having all things common or on the social control of the means and instruments of production! Such a system destroys the individual.

One of the fullest expositions of the realities of the profit motive and private enterprise found in the creeds of Christendom is in the Larger Catechism of the Westminster Confession of Faith and Catechisms. Question 140 reads:

"Which is the eighth commandment? A. The eighth commandment is, *Thou shalt not steal."*

Question 141:

"What are the duties required in the eighth commandment? A. The duties required in the eighth commandment are, truth, faithfulness, and justice in contracts and commerce between man and man; rendering to every one his due; restitution of goods unlawfully detained from the right owners thereof; giving and lending freely, according to our abilities, and the necessities of others; moderation of our judgments, wills, and affections, concerning worldly goods; a provident care and study to get, keep, use, and dispose of those things which are necessary and convenient for the sustentation of our nature, and suitable to our condition; a lawful calling, and diligence in it; frugality; avoiding unnecessary law-suits, and suretyship, or other like engagements; and an endeavor by all just and lawful means to procure, preserve, and further the wealth and outward estate of others, as well as our own."

In the phrase, "a provident care and study to get, keep, use, and dispose of those things which are necessary and convenient for the sustentation of our nature, and suitable to our condition," we have the profit motive described in a very full way. The relationship between man and his fellow man in the protection of his property is expressed in "justice in contracts and commerce between man and man." Here we see the whole free system of economy and the virtues that attend it. Many have never read this portion of the great Westminster Confession of Faith and Catechisms. There is not the slightest intimation here that things should be in common. Rather the reverse is true. The command asks us to help protect the estate of others, not to ask others to join with us in co-operative, common work of a socialistic order where the means of production will be in the hands of all for the good of all.

The opposite side of this picture is given to us in Question 142:

> "*What are the sins forbidden in the eighth command-ment? A.* The sins forbidden in the eighth commandment, beside the neglect of the duties required, are, theft, rob-bery, man-stealing, and receiving any thing that is stolen; fraudulent dealing, false weights and measures, removing land-marks, injustice and unfaithfulness in contracts be-tween man and man, or in matters of trust; oppression, extortion, usury, bribery, vexatious law-suits, unjust en-closures and depopulations: engrossing commodities to enhance the price, unlawful callings, and all other unjust or sinful ways of taking or withholding from our neigh-bour what belongs to him, or of enriching ourselves; covetousness, inordinate prizing and affecting worldly goods; distrustful and distracting cares and studies in get-ting, keeping, and using them; envying at the prosperity of others; as likewise idleness, prodigality, wasteful gam-ing; and all other ways whereby we do unduly prejudice our own outward estate: and defrauding ourselves of the due use and comfort of that estate which God hath given us."

Everything here is designed to protect and establish men in the use of the profit motive in private enterprise. The view of the individual involved in this exposition of the commandment is that of a free individual in a free economy, and it is sinful and wrong to take from him what belongs to him.

It has been the custom in many of the great reformed denominations that use the Larger and Shorter Catechisms to furnish proof texts in the catechism for each particular item mentioned.

The Shorter Catechism of the Westminster Confession of Faith used to be memorized by most of the boys and girls in Presbyterian Sunday schools and homes, and the practice is still observed in some places. Question 74 says:

> "*What is required in the eighth commandment? A.* The eighth commandment requireth the lawful procuring and furthering the wealth and outward estate of ourselves and others."

One of the proof texts that is given in support of this question is 2 Thessalonians 3:10-12: "For even when we were with you, this we commanded you, that if any would not work, neither should he eat. For we hear that there are some which walk among you disorderly, working not at all, but are busybodies. Now them that are such we command and exhort by our Lord Jesus Christ, that with quietness they work, and eat their own bread." This is a text that is twisted beyond all means and measure by those who desire to find a communistic hint in it. Paul is saying that if there are those in our midst who refuse to work, the people should not give them food. These are the people who are walking disorderly and causing trouble, and the apostle issued a command "by our Lord Jesus Christ, that with quietness they work, and eat their own bread," not the communal bread, not the bread that is the product of their consumer-co-operatives. Private enterprise is here commanded, and the Catechism puts it, "The lawful procuring and furthering the wealth and outward estate of ourselves." "Lawful" means in contrast to stealing, or the communistic estate. The profit motive is here again verified.

There is another and an exceedingly interesting angle by which this is also approached in the Westminster Confession of Faith and Catechisms. It is Chapter XXIII, "Of the Civil Magistrate," which reads:

> "God, the Supreme Lord and King of all the world, hath ordained civil magistrates to be under him over the people, for his own glory and the public good, and to this end, hath armed them with the power of the sword, for the defence and encouragement of them that are good, and for the punishment of evil doers."

What is the basis on which society is to punish the evildoers? By what norm does it determine evildoers, those who violate God's law—steal, rob, plunder, and other violations of the rights of property? The Government is to protect the individual in his property, not to organize itself in such a way that the individual will have no opportunity to express the profit motive, as in the "peace through co-operatives" idea. Certainly the "evil doers" mentioned here are not those who are pronounced evildoers in a communistic order where anyone who disrupts or disturbs the fulfillment of the economic plan must be liquidated. But the Confession of Faith goes farther, and in Section III of this same chapter we read:

> "It is the duty of civil magistrates to protect the person and good name of all their people, in such an effectual manner as that no person be suffered, either upon pretence of religion or infidelity, to offer any indignity, violence, abuse, or injury to any other person whatsoever."

In other words, a government that will maintain, protect, and establish the rights of the individual in the exercise of the profit motive in lawful pursuits of gain will have the blessing of God. It derived its power from God. This is set in bold contrast to the collectivistic conception of the society itself becoming the lord and determiner of the individual's welfare, position, and security.

The choicest chapter of all in any of the confessions of faith is the one dealing with the liberty of conscience; and, as we have previously pointed out, it is only in an uncontrolled economic order that men can be free to work, gain, and give of their substance as they believe God wants them to do.

"God alone is Lord of the conscience, and hath left it free from the doctrines and commandments of men which are in any thing contrary to his word, or beside it in matters of faith or worship. So that to believe such doctrines, or to obey such commandments out of conscience, is to betray true liberty of conscience; and the requiring an implicit faith, and an absolute and blind obedience, is to destroy liberty of conscience, and reason also" (Chapter XX, Section II).

And it is in the collectivistic society, where the "common good" becomes supreme and absolute, that "blind obedience" is required. The destruction of freedom of speech, freedom of the press, and other civil liberties is brought about in order that by a controlled propaganda the obedience will not appear to be blind, but that the people will willingly obey because they have no better information. By such a catastrophe "liberty of conscience, and reason" are destroyed. A society that does not permit liberty of conscience cannot be a free society.

Martin Luther prepared what is known as "Luther's Small Catechism," in which he discussed in one question the command, "Thou shalt not steal." He gave us the same emphasis and statement that we have seen in the Westminster Shorter Catechism,

"We should so fear and love God as not to take our neighbor's money or property, nor get it by false ware or dealing, but help him to improve and protect his property and livelihood."

This is the property right that is inherent in the profit motive and necessitates a free society.

The Heidelberg Catechism, 1563, used in many Reformed Churches, considers this eighth commandment.

"What does God forbid in the eighth commandment? Answer: Not only such theft and robbery as are punished by the magistrate, but God views as theft also all wicked tricks and devices whereby we seek to draw to ourselves our neighbor's goods, whether by force or with show of right, such as unjust weights, ells, measures, wares, coins, usury, or any means forbidden of God; so, moreover, all covetousness, and all useless waste of his gifts."

The next question asks:

"But what does God require of thee in this commandment? Answer: That I further my neighbor's good where I can and may, deal with him as I would have others deal with me, and labor faithfully that I may be able to help the poor in their need."

The right of property is an eternal right. It is a perpetual right grounded in the moral nature of God and revealed to us in His command, "Thou shalt not steal."

There is an interesting phrase in what is called the French Confession of Faith of 1559. Its last sentence reads:

"Therefore we detest all those who would like to reject authority, to establish community and confusion of property, and overthrow the order of justice."

The men who prepared and wrote these creeds certainly would reject the modern church with its emphasis upon the placing of the means of production in the hands of all. They would oppose it because the Bible is opposed to any community, and therefore confusion, of property.

There are many other creeds that could be quoted, but the ones that we have given are from the Episcopal, the Methodist, the Reformed, the Presbyterian, and the Lutheran Churches. These are certainly sufficient to establish our contention that the creeds of the historic Christian church support private enterprise. The creeds say one thing; the Bible and the creeds agree, but the modern church says the opposite.

One prevalent expression, which is very popular in the modern church, helps to explain the dilemma in which we find ourselves: "No creed, but a life." We have been told from thousands of pulpits that we are not interested in dead, outworn creeds; we are interested in a life. Other men have thought that when they simply pointed out the fallacy of this slogan,—that a life without faith is not possible, just as an apple without the apple tree is not possible,—they had gone far enough in blocking the attack. But the effects of the attack can be seen when one realizes that it has discouraged even the reading of the creeds, much less the understanding of them. As a result, people do not know what they believe and do not know what their church is supposed to believe. Therefore, when men arise to preach their sermons, robed in the dignity of the clergy and the sanctity of the pulpit, and they talk about "brotherhood" and replacing the profit motive with some higher and more noble motive such as co-operation or service, people do not realize that they are having offered to them, in the name of Christianity, the very heart of the Marxian philosophy. Nor do they realize that everything we hold dear in our free society has been abandoned by the preacher when he thus exhorts.

An outstanding example of the influence of this kind of preaching upon the life of lay America was furnished when, in the Waldorf-Astoria Hotel, January 31, 1945, John D. Rockefeller, Jr., made an address to a group of outstanding Protestant leaders in the United States. He decried creeds and said that we need the life instead, and in his appeal for the rebirth of the church he said that such a reborn church "would pronounce ordinance, ritual, creed, all nonessential for admission into the Kingdom of God or His church. A life, not a creed, would be the test."

The attack upon the creeds has opened the way for the modern church to wage its campaign against the profit motive and private enterprise, and men like John D. Rockefeller, Jr., of all men, are helping the cause. The application of the philosophy that John D. Rockefeller, Jr., was promoting, and which is held by the very Protestant leaders to whom he was speaking, would never have permitted the society in which John D. Rockefeller, Jr., came into his present estate. The liberal leaders in the Federal Council who realize the import of what they are advocating must get a great deal of satisfaction out of having a man like John D. Rockefeller, Jr.'s being used, as he is, to advance their cause. And how many thousand other good sincere believers in private enterprise are unwittingly doing the same thing?

The divergence of the modern church's message from the

plain teaching of its own creeds, however, raises a number of questions. How does the church justify and explain this departure from its creeds? The church's creeds say one thing and the Federal Council is proclaiming another. Is this not hypocrisy? Yea, is it not even dishonesty? These ministers and bishops take their oath promising allegiance to the Confession and the Articles of Religion. How do they justify this contradiction? How do they explain it? These are the questions we should like answered! There are some answers given us. For instance, we are told that times are different, that the church is growing and finding a fuller expression of truth. Others have attempted to obscure the dishonesty by saying that the church at this time is moving on to a slightly different emphasis from what it had at the time the creed was adopted; or, that the creeds do have an historic value, and should be preserved because of that. Surely the Social Creed of the Churches considered in Chapter 5 and the historic creeds of Christendom considered here are from different religions. Is not the church supposed, in all honesty, to be true to its witness and creed? Of course it is, and such is the basic matter that is involved. It is this same dishonesty that has made treaties between nations scraps of paper, and that leaves the door wide open for Stalin to scrap any of his present agreements when he sees fit. This is the general demoralization that plagues us everywhere today.

It is not a question of the church's moving on into fuller knowledge. It is a question as to what the Bible teaches. The teaching of the Bible about the individual, to whom the church is to bear testimony, has not changed one iota. The validity of the command, "Thou shalt not steal," gives us the profit motive and the private enterprise system; it has not been changed since the day God gave it to Moses on the Mount; or better still, since the moment of the creation of the world. The crime of the church in departing from its creed is a crime against God and against Heaven.

These great churches inside the Federal Council have been built up through the period of the life and history of this country. Property, endowments—millions upon millions of dollars—have gone into them out of the pockets of men and women who believed that the church stood for the things that its creed proclaimed. All of this property has been given to the church for the presentation of the revealed system of truth which protects the individual; and now these very churches, these millions, their publishing houses, and all the rest, are being used to proclaim the philosophy that the private enterprise system, the profit motive, must be replaced by the "service and co-operative motive." It represents, in our opinion, one of the most colossal steals of all time. The enemies of the church have come in and taken over, and are using the resources of the church against the very thing it was established to teach!

If the leaders of the modern church are proclaiming doctrines contrary to the creed, how about the church itself? Is it being true to its creed? The answer is that the living organism of the church is made up of the ministers and the groups that are now controlling it, and they have no disposition to use their influence for purifying and bringing their present-day organism into accord with the creed. The creed is a scrap of paper, a relic of bygone days of battle. But there is considerably more involved than just the church. It is the people. As goes the church, so goes the nation. It is in this particular that we would ask the question, "Which way, America—private enterprise or a controlled economy?" The church has deserted its creed. It has deserted the plain teaching of the Scriptures; it is asking us to change to a collectivistic, controlled social order in the very hour when the nation has spent its billions, obligating us and our children to protect our system of freedom.

What caused these preachers and the church to depart? This is a question we shall discuss after we have looked at a number of matters that are very closely related to the creeds, such as the real freedom of democracy and the true freedom of labor.

CHAPTER 11

THE BILL OF RIGHTS

IF THE United States ever loses its free economy, it will be lost in the name of democracy. It is on this appeal that the leaders of the church are gaining recruits for their march of tomorrow on the citadel of freedom. It is in the terms "industrial democracy" and "economic democracy" that the Federal Council has advocated revolutionary social change. The bombs to blow our citadel of freedom to bits are being carried and unsuspectedly distributed among individuals of the land. Nearly all of the leftist organizations in the United States are operating under the title of "democracy" in some form or other.

Lenin called the new Soviet power "the proletarian democracy" when he submitted his "Theses and Report" to the first congress of the Third International. He said it was "attracting the mass organization of the working people to permanent and unconditional participation in the conduct of the government."

Karl Marx was equally as insistent upon the use of the word "democracy" and "democratic principles." In a letter written May 5, 1875, to Wilhelm Bracke, Marx said concerning the transition from capitalism to communism:

"Only in communist society, when the resistance of the capitalists has finally been broken, when the capitalists have disappeared, when there are no longer any classes (that is, when there is no difference between the members of society in respect of their social means of production), only then ... 'can one speak of freedom.' Only then will a really full democracy, a democracy without any exceptions be possible and be realized."

The word as we use it means one thing; but, as Marx uses it, it means something entirely different. It is in this different understanding of the words "democracy" and "liberty," as they are used on one side by those who believe in collectivism and the Russian way and on the other side by those of us who believe in individualism and the American way, that the struggle between the two ideas is raging.

There ought not to be any confusion, but there is. Many people think that when these revolutionary leaders use the word "democracy" they are talking about the same thing that we believe democracy to be. They listen and are led to believe that democracy is supposed to do things for them which, according to our American understanding, it was never intended to do. It is in the confusion produced by the different concepts of these words that the rise of the tyrant may be obscured.

America loves her Bill of Rights. The Constitution of the United States is our bulwark of freedom. So long as that Constitution stands, not merely in words, but also in spirit, we shall have freedom. When, by the sudden death of the late President Franklin Delano Roosevelt, the President, Harry Truman, in the providence of God was brought so quickly to the highest office in our land, he placed his hand, as every President before him has done, upon the Holy Bible, and took the solemn oath of office, which reads:

"I do solemnly swear (or affirm) that I will faithfully execute the office of President of the United States, and will, to the best of my ability, preserve, protect, and defend the Constitution of the United States."

The concept of liberty that Americans hold is given and specifically defined for them in the Bill of Rights. This is our charter. This alone is liberty to us; this alone is liberty for mankind. There are not two different kinds of liberty, the Russian kind and the American kind. There is only one system of liberty, and God, in His gracious providence and mercy, has given that system to the United States in her charter of freedom.

This is the most individualistic document ever written by the pen of man. This produced American individualism. This is capitalism's charter.

Only in an economically free society can the amendment to the Constitution mean anything:

"Congress shall make no law respecting an establishment of religion, or prohibiting the free exercise thereof; or abridging the freedom of speech or of the press; or the right of the people peaceably to assemble and to petition the Government for a redress of grievances."

Thus the individual's right stands out above all other rights. Furthermore, Articles IX and X tell us:

"The enumeration in the Constitution of certain rights shall not be construed to deny or disparage others retained by the people." "The powers not delegated to the United States by the Constitution, nor prohibited by it to the States, are reserved to the States respectively, or to the people."

The powers of the State are limited and defined. The individual alone is free.

In this charter the individual's rights stand above the power of the State, and the individual's rights are limited here only in the most specific possible way for the securing of the welfare of society. But the individualism implied here is more specifically stated in the fifth article of the Bill of Rights:

> "No person shall be . . . deprived of life, liberty, or property, without due process of law; nor shall private property be taken for public use without just compensation."

Here life and property—the one dealing with the command, "Thou shalt not kill," and the other dealing with the command, "Thou shalt not steal"—are put into the same classification, and protected by our law. The individual is entitled to his property because it is his. If its public use should be desired, there must be just compensation, a recognition of his ownership of it, and the value of it. This involves the profit motive, the individual's gain of his property, and the whole system of individualism that is in such disrepute in the Federal Council's propaganda.

Whence did this idea of the property rights of the individual come? As we saw in the last chapter, it came from the creeds of the church. The same conception of the individual, the same realm of truth embodied in those pronouncements, is here incorporated in the Constitution of the United States.

In the amendments is another article that emphasizes these things. It is Article IV:

> "The right of the people to be secure in their persons, houses, papers, and effects, against unreasonable searches and seizures, shall not be violated, and no warrants shall issue but upon probable cause, supported by oath or affirmation, and particularly describing the place to be searched, and the persons or things to be seized."

Only "upon probable cause, supported by oath," can the power of Government be used to call in question a man's property or person. It is in the freedom given to man under this amendment that we have free enterprise—individuals working, profiting, succeeding. But these matters are in the Constitution of the United States not merely because they are in the creeds of the historic Christian church, but mainly and primarily because they are written in the Word of God. The Constitution of the United States clearly sets forth the Bible's position concerning the individual. What a blessing! How we ought to thank our forefathers for such a heritage! How we ought constantly to thank the Almighty God!

We have reached a point now where our logic and our facts demand that we see clearly one of the most significant facts concerning the attack of the modern church upon private enterprise. If the Constitution of the United States, as we have seen, guarantees the right of the individual; if this right comes from the creeds of the historic Christian Church, as we have proved; and if this truth lives in the Word of God, as the Bible testifies, then the attack of the modern church upon the profit motive and individualism is an attack in its whole scope upon the ideology set forth in the Constitution of the United States. It is an attack upon the Constitution in the most subtle and serious possible fashion, and the sooner the Christian people of the country know it the better.

When, for instance, Dr. E. Stanley Jones, as we saw in Chapter 7, tells us that we must take the fullest expression of freedom, as we have it in the United States, and the best expression of collectivism, as we have it in Russia, and blend the two in the creation of a "new man," something entirely different, what does that do to the Constitution of the United States?

When the Federal Council goes to Cleveland and conducts its second study session on a just and durable peace, and, as the Michigan editor says, "lugged in by the heels" this attack upon private property, what does that do to the Constitution of the United States?

The concept of freedom set forth in the Constitution of the United States, however, is under attack from another sector of the same front, under the terms "economic democracy," "industrial democracy," "economic freedom." This attack is varied and exceedingly subtle. Economic freedom is put in contrast to political freedom. We are told that we have a political Bill of Rights in the Constitution, and we must now have an economic bill of rights. Such a contrast is fallacious and disastrous. The preamble to the Constitution reads:

> "We, the people of the United States, in order to form a more perfect Union, establish justice, insure domestic tranquillity, provide for the common defence, promote the general welfare, and secure the blessings of liberty to ourselves and our posterity, do ordain and establish this CONSTITUTION for the United States of America."

The Constitution is an instrument of liberty, for liberty. It is not only political liberty that is guaranteed here, but also individual liberty. His economic liberty is guaranteed; his civil liberty is guaranteed; his political liberty is guaranteed; his religious liberty is guaranteed; his liberty of speech is guaranteed. It is a document that exalts individualism as it has never before been exalted in the history of Government. The individual is free. Because of the declaration of this preamble, America has had the blessings of liberty, and we have grown to be the most powerful nation on the face of the earth. Furthermore, we are told that "no person [singular] shall be . . . deprived of . . . liberty . . . without due process of law."

But this economic democracy which would give us a State-planned or a group-controlled economy, this economic democracy, which, according to the co-operatives, puts the ownership of the means and instruments of production in the hands of all, is absolutely foreign to the whole idea of the Constitution. This is the reason we must stand our ground and not yield to compromises with the Russian system! This will be the greatest temptation and peril of our post-war world.

The idea of the Government's going into business to compete with the individual and thus restricting his life, liberty, and property is foreign to the purpose and spirit of the amendments. The idea of Government ownership of the economic processes in which the individual's property would be jeopardized is absolutely foreign to the Constitution. If these matters are ever to be injected into the Constitution, they will have to come by means of radical amendments, or they may come by means of Congress, under the leadership of the President, embarking upon a controlled political economy and the United States Supreme Court upholding the matter and interpreting it as being constitutional. This would cause the destruction of the Constitution by nullification, the most probable and likely way in which it will come, if it ever does. God forbid! And the third, of course, is the way of bloody revolution, overthrowing our Government by force.

In the Federal Council's program, according to its various literature, the last thought the leaders have is that their desired changes in the basic structure of our social order should come by violence or force. Nothing could be farther from their purpose. They want the changes to come by the orderly processes of democracy. We can vote these things into being by the election of Congressmen who will embrace these planned economy ideas; then if men in the Supreme Court should be sympathetic to planned economy, the whole thing could be declared constitutional under the expanding idea of the Constitution as a living document. The Constitution *is* a living document, and will continue to be so as long as its first duty is to preserve liberty; but it will cease to live when the protection it gives to the individual, to his life and property, is swallowed in the collectivistic notions of a socially controlled economy. We have our economic Bill of Rights in the present Bill of Rights of the Constitution. We need no other, because this is grounded on the Word of God.

The so-called "economic democracy" is not democracy at all. Lenin and Marx may speak of it as democracy. Lenin said that it gave to the people a "permanent and unconditional participation in the conduct of the Government," and he was right. It is so permanent and unconditional that the individual is denied his own liberty, the expression of his own initiative, the development of his own personality and conscience. He is permanently and unconditionally a part of the plan, and though he may vote against the plan, though he may not like the plan, he has no minority rights of dissent. Dissent means nothing. In other words, such an economic democracy does not have a valid minority. It has to become a one-party system, or it cannot survive.

Democracy does not exist unless there are minority rights, and a minority does not exist if it is silenced by the will and force of the majority. The Russian Constitution describes it a little more accurately in the phrase, "the dictatorship of the proletariat." In such a dictatorship, call it democracy if you will, there are no minority privileges or rights. If the minority were privileged to have a plan of its own, or refused to go along with the plan established, the majority's plan would collapse.

But there is a far more basic reason why this is not democracy. It destroys the individual upon which democracy depends. Free, representative democracy—a republic—is absolutely dependent upon an educated, enlightened, free citizenry. When the citizenry becomes enslaved in any manner whatsoever, even if that slavery be injected on a portion of the group by the overbearing power of a capitalistic exploiter, democracy is a farce. It would be better today if we used the word "republic" more than we do, when we speak of our form of government, for that is what we have. If you destroy the freedom of the individual, you destroy democracy. Destroy the freedom of the individual, and you destroy the profit motive. When the leaders of the Federal Council tell us that the whole basis of society must be changed, we, in the light of the Constitution of the United States, see the import of it. The Constitution which guarantees our way of life must be changed; the attack is upon it. If more Christians realized this, they would not be so profuse in their approval of leaders like Dr. E. Stanley Jones and Dr. G. Bromley Oxnam. They would readily warn people against their false teachings.

CHAPTER 12

THE FREEDOM TO LABOR

OUR American democracy has been built upon the individual, and what we call equal opportunity. Each man is free to go out and labor where he pleases. He may run a grocery store. He may work for somebody else. He may quit one employer, if he pleases, and go to work for another. Individual talents and what we call the "bent" of a man have room for expression, according to his desire and calling. If a man wants to be a carpenter, a plumber, a baker, a butcher; if he wants to follow the trade of his father; if, instead, he would rather be a doctor, or a preacher, he is free to make such a decision for himself and put out his shingle. He may succeed, or he may fail.

America today is flooded with the stories of men who started at the bottom and have gone to the top, who began with nothing and have become men of means and influence. We have had a land of freedom, and the man who should appreciate this freedom more than any other individual is the hard-working laboring man. If he reaches that stage in life where he begins to feel that he has failed, that he has let his opportunities slip, he can at least know that his son or his grandson has a chance to "get on in life." He does not have to reconcile himself to his son's being a cog in some regimented order or moved about at the will of the planners in some collectivistic utopia. America's greatest treasure is liberty.

The one man, however, who is being deceived in this matter of liberty, perhaps more than any other person, is the laborer, the member of a union. The propaganda used, for instance, by Mr. James Myers, as we saw in Chapter 5, is designed to mislead the laborer and make him think he is getting something when he is actually being led to embrace the idea that individualism and individual ownership are neither profitable nor right. He is being misled; first, because he is fed on propaganda that inflames class hatred in America, hatred of the capitalist, hatred of management, hatred of those who have money; second, because he is being told that the way to get even with those who have prospered is to destroy the system that makes it possible for them to succeed. But the destruction of the system will make it impossible also for this man, his children, and his children's children to get gain.

The sustained program of the Federal Council is being offered to the laboring man, though the Federal Council does declare that it is desirous of helping the industrialist and the owner of private enterprise. But the effect is actually to embitter, to stir hatred; and it does so. To hear some people talk, a man today who owns anything is the enemy of society; at least, so it would appear. Although many of these men have come up the hard, long road, not working just eight hours, not watching a union clock, but struggling all hours of the day and night, sacrificing comforts and pleasures in order that they may get ahead, their wealth must be taken away from them and distributed to others.

The Federal Council denounces anti-Semitism, but it promotes anti-capitalism. The Federal Council repudiates anti-racialism, singling out the colored man, but it is fanning the flame of class hatred, telling the laboring man that he is in a separate class, an oppressed class. America has never been a land of classes. By the way, the remedy that the Federal Council has for the anti-race problem is just as absurd and ridiculous as the one it has for the solution of our economic problems, the destruction of the profit motive. Its propaganda logically will destroy the races. The way to be rid of anti-racialism is to destroy the races themselves. We cannot go into that subject in this treatise, but it is a tremendously significant field because the Federal Council propaganda is only aggravating the matter, not solving it. America is a land of free men, and it is the enjoyment of the exercise of freedom and the maintenance and defense of freedom that make us a classless society.

We, in a true sense, are all workers and servants, from the President who serves the nation to the person who mops the White House floors. In America all work; lawful enterprise is honorable! There is no class.

It is because there are those who feel that the labor movement can be used for the destruction of our system of private enterprise, that radical leaders and the communist elements have gotten into the labor movement to lead it and use it as an instrument for the revolution. Undoubtedly, this is the reason the Federal Council's radical leadership, realizing the full significance of their attack upon the profit motive and their offering of a planned economy, turned to labor as a fertile field for their quick development. Labor has a respected and honored place in America. We are all laboring men; and we all have to live and learn our lessons in the great school of hard knocks.

The right of contract is one of the most precious rights of private enterprise. A man may agree to work for another for a stipulated amount and receive his wages; or several men may join and make such an agreement. It is this joining in agreement that is the basis for the legalizing of collective bargaining. This is not socialism, not for a minute. John

Stuart Mill in his eminent essay, "On Liberty," states it this way:

> "From this liberty of each individual, follows the liberty, within the same limits, of combination among individuals; freedom to unite, for any purpose not involving harm to others" (p. 28).

But labor will not stop at its collective bargaining gains. It is into the fields of collective control and collective ownership that labor is being baited and led, and this will inevitably bring chaos and with it the destruction of our free enterprise.

The principle of the closed shop is a totalitarian principle in labor. The uniting in the "closed" shop harms others. John Stuart Mill's analysis is right. For a group of laboring men to form themselves into a union and say to another man, "You cannot work with us; in fact, you cannot work at this trade or in this shop or any other shop where our men operate unless you join us," is the principle of the highjacker who puts a pistol into a man's ribs and says, "Come with me, or I'll shoot!" The "closed shop" becomes the weapon of power! In a free country where individuals give an account of themselves to God, a man ought to be free to join a union if he desires, but, if for some conscientious reason he does not want to join, the men in the closed shop, because they are larger and stronger, have no right to crush him or to refuse to permit him to work.

Oh, yes, they say, "There are other plants that are not unionized, that are not closed shops, where you can work." But just wait until this union or closed shop idea covers all the fields of industry! There are certain fields today where the union has a complete monopoly. There, men cannot work at the trade they have learned and in which they are skilled unless they join the union. What the men who are so insistent upon the closed shop fail to realize is that the same tyranny they exercise toward their fellow laborer in refusing to permit him to work, they are creating for the destruction of themselves and the hindrance of their own development and growth. It is this tyranny that will give them the collectivistic order in which the union will become their master and tyrant. When they work for private enterprise, they are free to leave and work elsewhere; but, when the unions get control, men will not be free to leave, and the laboring man will be enslaved by the octopus of his own creation. Has the laboring man forgotten that Russia is one closed shop? The men in Russia can never work for any other union. There is no other employer to whom they can go; freedom has left the land.

The man who desires to join a union must respect the right and liberty of the man who does not want to join. The union should win its members on the basis of its own merit and not by a club—the closed shop. Liberty assumes the exercise of reason by reasonable men, and when this is excluded from the sphere of operation tyranny is enthroned. It is not for the union to tell a man what is best for him— that is, that he has to join it in order to work. The concept of the union involved in the closed shop needs to be reexamined. Shall a man refuse to work beside another man simply because the man has not joined his guild? This is not America, the land of free men with equal opportunity. The man who does not want to join a union has as much right to work and as much right to refuse to be coerced as has the man who joins. If not, there will be freedom for the union man in America and no freedom for the nonunion man; this is not the American idea; it is the Russian concept. The seriousness of this condition cannot possibly be overemphasized.

Harry F. Ward, in his volume to which we have referred, "The Soviet Spirit," holds before us the wonders and the glories of this totalitarianism, and tells us that in it boys and girls graduating from controlled schools where they have been taught the lessons that totalitarianism wants them to learn do not have to wait for jobs, but the jobs are waiting for them; in fact, some of them begin working in these jobs before they are graduated. Yes, their jobs are assigned. Yes, they are moved about by the planning commission or committee. They are not free to live where they desire. They must live and work where their union has decided that the work should be done and where they are needed. The closed shop has in it all the principles of slavery—human slavery.

If our American way of freedom is to be preserved, the men in the unions, the individual laboring men of America, must put the liberty of the land above any temporary gain or what they may consider as personal gain. This does not mean that they should not use their right of collective bargaining to get better wages and better working conditions. A man, or a group of men, has a perfect right to say, "I'll work for you for so much if you will make the conditions such and such." A union is not wrong; and it may and can be an agency for real freedom! But when labor says, "You'll take our terms, or we'll destroy your business," it has become radical and destructive.

The Wagner Labor Act needs to be revised. It is too one-sided. It encourages labor to move into the collectivistic sphere of activity. The responsibility of the Government is to see that the fields of private enterprise, free economy, and competition are open, and when labor enters to monopolize, the same principle that was established in law in the

Sherman Anti-Trust Act needs to be put into effect with regard to labor. When private monopolies seek to control the economic sphere and destroy competition, Government can legitimately stop them. When, by the same token, labor unions seek to control, the Government has the same responsibility to restrict them. The legitimate restraints of Government upon society are the restraints that will keep society free. But labor knows that in this particular field it has many votes; it names its candidates and fights to get them elected. It is here that the activities of radical labor in the political field are so disastrous and have such far-reaching consequences for our American freedoms.

When the Political Action Committee, for instance, sends to Congress men who favor their radical ideas, involving the destruction of private enterprise and the establishment of a planned economy,—men sent by democratic processes—you have revolution taking place under the structure of our democratic setup. When labor once goes into politics, it uses its power not only to advance the position of labor but also to enter into a great many other spheres of activity. The Political Action Committee, for instance, under Sidney Hillman, is lined up with forces in the Federal Council to attempt to restrict the preaching of the Gospel on paid radio Gospel programs in the United States. This is where the danger is so patent. The Federal Council helps radical labor, giving it comfort and ammunition for its "economic democracy." So labor joins with the Federal Council to aid it in crushing the preaching of the historic Gospel of grace.

When the power of organized labor is used to destroy our system of free economy, then labor will find itself controlled by the planners. Labor will discover to its everlasting sorrow and shame that it has been responsible not only for the destruction of its own liberty but also for the liberties of all the American people. A responsibility, the like of which has not before rested upon any individual, is resting upon the laboring man in the unions today. He must stand for liberty, for our American system of private enterprise. He must refuse to be a party to what in the union would destroy his fellow American's right to work. But the laboring man will have to pay a price if he does stand for these American principles. He is apt to be slugged; someone working next to him may see that he is "accidentally" injured.

The ungodliness exercised by the union leaders in operating some of the unions is far worse than the ungodliness of the exploiter-capitalist. We do not advocate that the way to meet this problem is to destroy our system of free economy, nor do we believe that the unions should be put under a controlled economy as the Federal Council leaders have advocated in meeting the abuses in the management field in the handling of gains. In our opinion, the Christian laboring man has resting upon him today the greatest responsibility that has ever rested upon any single American. He is being flooded with all the propaganda that creates class hatred. He has about him the pressure to stand for the principles of totalitarianism in his "closed" union. This man must remember that, as he stands for liberty, unpopular and abused though he may be, he is doing as noble service for the cause and maintenance of our American way of life as the man who has died on the battlefield. If we lose the freedom to labor, we have lost our American freedom.

CHAPTER 13

THE REASON FOR TYRANNY

WE MUST now face one of the major questions that has been in the background as we have developed this discussion. In fact, this question will help to resolve the mystery of the conflict and the contradiction that appear before us. Why have these leaders in the modern church departed so far from the Scriptures that they attack the profit motive and depose the individual from the place God has given him in society? The creeds of the church say one thing about it; these men in their writings say another. The Constitution of the United States demands one thing; these leaders by their activities want another. What has caused them to go so far astray? Perhaps we had better let them speak for themselves.

The reason is at hand. They have gotten away from the one source of truth in which are maintained and exalted the great fundamentals upon which society rests—the Word of God. Yes, that is the tragedy, the supreme tragedy of this hour. The Bible has always been the rule, the infallible rule, of faith and practice. There, in times past, men read the commands of God and went out and obeyed them because they were God's. There men learned the great doctrines and accepted them because the Lord had spoken. But the situation is different now. The story of how the modern church, through these last fifty years, has gotten away from the historic position of the true church is a long, involved, and intricate one. It goes back, strange as it may seem, to the roots of higher criticism inside Germany. It has affected almost every church. Colleges, universities, seminaries—the whole educational world has been affected. We are reaping the fruits of unbelief, born in Germany and injected into the church. Germany really has reaped the whirlwind! We have discussed this question in our previous book, "Twentieth Century Reformation."

Let us permit Dr. Oxnam and Dr. Jones to testify for themselves. They will furnish us the evidence that will prove our point. They are leaders in the Protestant Church today.

One would naturally expect that in a book entitled, "Preaching in a Revolutionary Age," a collection of addresses delivered before young theological students, the speaker would tell them what they should preach and also intimate what they should not preach. The great burden of Dr. Oxnam's book is that the minister today must denounce the unbearable sin of such an unjust society, the inequality of which is a stench in the nostrils of Jehovah. In one passage, we find Dr. Oxnam taking real issue with God's denunciation of sin and His judgment. It is in this passage that one sees how completely Dr. Oxnam has broken with the historic Christian faith.

"Hugh Walpole, in *Wintersmoon,* tells of a father and son at church. The aged rector read from the Old Testament, and the boy learned of the terrible God who sent plagues upon the people and created fiery serpents to assault them. That night, when the father passed the boy's bedroom, the boy called him, put his arms around his father's neck, and, drawing him close, said, 'Father, you hate Jehovah. So do I. I loathe him, dirty bully!' We have long since rejected a conception of reconciliation associated historically with an ideal of a Deity that is loathsome. God, for us, cannot be thought of as an angry, awful, avenging Being who because of Adam's sin must have his

Shylockian pound of flesh. No wonder the honest boy in justifiable repugnance could say, 'Dirty bully' " (p. 79).

This ought to shock every Christian. The modern church has gone so far as to make fun of Adam's sin and original sin; yet this is the very foundation of the Bible's doctrine of sin and its consequences. Paul tells us in Romans 5:12, 17-19: "By one man sin entered into the world, and death by sin; and so death passed upon all men, for that all have sinned. . . . By one man's offence death reigned. . . . Therefore as by the offence of one judgment came upon all men to condemnation. . . . By one man's disobedience many were made sinners."

The Methodist Articles of Religion contain an entire section dealing with the sin of Adam. Article VII:

"Of Original or Birth Sin.

"Original sin standeth not in the following of Adam (as the Pelagians do vainly talk), but it is the corruption of the nature of every man, that naturally is engendered of the offspring of Adam, whereby man is very far gone from original righteousness, and of his own nature inclined to evil, and that continually."

"The wages of sin is death." Think of Dr. Oxnam's picturing God as Shylockian! God's Word has this to say as to His being angry, "The wrath of God is revealed from heaven against all ungodliness and unrighteousness" (Rom. 1:18); as to His being awful, "It is a fearful thing to fall into the hands of the living God" (Heb. 10:31); as to His being avenging, "Vengeance is mine," He declares; "I will repay" (Rom. 12:19). Consider such a verse as John 3:36, "He that believeth on the Son hath everlasting life: and he that believeth not the Son shall not see life; but the wrath of God [the anger of God] abideth on him." The reason man needs a Redeemer, the reason he must be reconciled, is that he is at enmity with God. Think of Dr. Oxnam, a bishop in the Methodist Church, telling us that "we have long since rejected a conception of reconciliation associated historically with an ideal of a Deity that is loathsome"! Of course, the natural mind loathes such a God of wrath. It is because the Christian church has believed in the historical record which presents to us a God who is angry, a God whose law has been flouted, that men are ready to proclaim the offer of reconciliation that God Himself has made through Jesus Christ. Think of a Methodist bishop's speaking of the God of Adam as a "dirty bully"! This is near to blasphemy!

But how about the plagues? They were acts of judgment upon the people because of their sin. Then he speaks of the fiery serpents which God created to assault the people. That reference is one to which our own Redeemer refers in John 3:14, 15: "As Moses lifted up the serpent in the wilderness, even so must the Son of man be lifted up: that whosoever believeth in him should not perish, but have eternal life." The fiery serpents came in judgment for the people's sin, their violation of God's commandments. And God, by Moses, erected in their midst a brazen serpent, and told Moses to command the people that whoever would look upon that serpent God would heal and save. So today God has commanded that the terrible God of wrath and judgment will become a gracious God of love and life to everyone who will lift up his eyes to His Son, whom He has lifted up upon the cross of Calvary, and believe that He is the Redeemer for their sins.

Here we have clearly compacted into one paragraph the real reason why the modern church has drifted away. Unbelief is the only word that can explain it. Dr. Oxnam used

the words "long since rejected." He tells young preachers
to denounce the sin of a society in which the profit motive
exists; he then warns them against the "dirty bully" idea of
God, the terrible God who, because of Adam's sin, pro-
nounced death upon the race. If the race did not fall in
Adam's sin, then it could not be saved in the second federal
Head, the Lord Jesus Christ. Does not the very reading of
Dr. Oxnam's words make you cringe?

The Bible also gives us a text or two that explain for us
exactly what has happened in the modern church that it
offers to us a planned economy. We find one of these verses
in Jeremiah 6:19: "Hear, O earth: behold, I will bring evil
upon this people, even the fruit of their thoughts, because
they have not hearkened unto my words, nor to my law, but
rejected it." The collectivistic idea of a controlled economy
is the fruit of the thoughts of men who have "rejected"
God's conception of reconciliation. This section of Jeremiah
gives us the whole picture of the study in a very few sen-
tences. Verse 16 says the "old paths" will bring blessing and
rest. "Thus saith the Lord, Stand ye in the ways, and see, and
ask for the old paths, where is the good way, and walk
therein, and ye shall find rest for your souls." This includes
the security of the teaching of God's law on private enterprise. We have been blessed above all nations!

When we no longer accept God's thoughts, then we have
evil—"the fruit of their thoughts." We no longer have the
favor of God. "To what purpose cometh there to me incense
from Sheba, and the sweet cane from a far country? your
burnt-offerings are not acceptable, nor your sacrifices sweet
unto me" (v. 20).

But God turns against us, and we have certain trouble.
"Therefore thus saith the Lord, Behold, I will lay stumbling
blocks before this people, and the fathers and the sons to-

gether shall fall upon them; the neighbour and his friend shall perish" (v. 21). Yes, indeed, America has a stumbling block today. It is the ideology of "collectivism"—Russia. How we have already "stumbled" in dealing with her! If we stay by God's Word, we shall have rest—God will give it to us; if we do not, we shall "stumble," fathers and sons together, and our neighbors and friends shall suffer because of our fall.

When one sees a thing like this so confirmed in the Scriptures themselves, it helps to strengthen his faith. The Bible is true. These are indeed days for Jeremiahs. In Chapter 7, we read of God's declaring, "Walk ye in all the ways that I have commanded you, that it may be well unto you. But they hearkened not, nor inclined their ear, but walked in the counsels and in the imagination of their evil heart, and went backward, and not forward" (vs. 23, 24). It is backward we are now going, too! If we walk in the system of free enterprise and the profit motive, as it is given to us in the Scriptures, it will be well with us. But if we walk in the counsels and the imaginations of an evil heart—the system produced from the heart of those who reject the truth of God, the controlled economy—God declares that we shall go backward and not forward. Backward—yes, into slavery!

The reason for tyranny is the rejection of God's Word. When men reject the light of God's Word, they turn to the darkness of death for their brief existence here on earth. The Christian religion is one system—a deposit, the oracles of God; the Marxist ideology garbed in Christian terminology is another.

Dr. E. Stanley Jones, in his book, gives us a passage or two that are of a little different nature from those that Dr. Oxnam gives, but yet which serve to support this present point in an exceptionally fine manner. Dr. Jones speaks of the fundamentalist-modernist controversy, and offers a solution for it.

"The Church has failed to bring to a living synthesis differing emphases within itself. Take the fundamentalist-modernist split—for it is a real split, a rift going straight through American Christianity. If the Church had a real grip on the absolute Person embodying the absolute Order, it would have been able to see, in the light of this all-encompassing conception, that both fundamentalism and modernism belong to the Kingdom, 'like a householder who produces what is new [modernism] and what is old [fundamentalism] from his stores,' and that both emphases are necessary" (p. 220).

We are indeed grateful that Dr. Jones recognizes that the rift running throughout American Christianity is real; and in our opinion it is because of this and this alone that there is real hope for our system of private enterprise and free economy in America. The differences between fundamentalism and modernism are not matters that can be reconciled. The fundamentalist says he believes in the atoning death of Christ; the modernist says he does not. The fundamentalist says he believes in the bodily resurrection of Christ from the dead; the modernist calls it a theory. The fundamentalist says he believes in the fall of Adam; the modernist calls it the conception of a "dirty bully." These are the eternal differences between truth and error. A modernism that produces a social order that is controlled and planned is impossible of reconciliation with the Christianity that produces a free economy. But Dr. Jones' solution of the conflict between fundamentalists and modernists is merely a further extension of his new man idea, as we saw it applied to the free economy and to the collectivistic economy. He simply says that both elements need to move on out and become one new man together.

After speaking of the fight between the two groups, he declares:

> "I am persuaded that if either one wins there will be planned revenge and continuing conflict. The only hope is that we can get each to change and come to a third position beyond each, gathering up the truth in each and eliminating the wrong in each—a new man out of both parties. That will make peace—the peace not of compromise but of comprehension. Then instead of the fundamentalist or the modernist will emerge the Christian" (p. 222).

Of all absurd and impossible ideas—that the fundamentalist, the man who believes in the atoning death of Christ, should join with the modernist, the man who denies the atoning death of Christ, and both of them emerge the Christian! It is like saying that light and darkness should join together and both of them emerge pure light. The fallacy of Dr. Jones' thinking lies in the fact that the fundamentalist is the Christian and the modernist who denies the saving doctrines of the Scripture is not a Christian. He is absolutely right when he speaks about the struggle going on. This conflict, the conflict between Christ and Antichrist, between the eternal truth of God and the darkness of hell and Satan, has been raging since the day that Adam fell.

One outstanding departure from the Word of God is Dr. Jones' use of the words, "new man." The new man of Scripture is the supernaturally "born again" man. "Except a man be born again, he cannot see the kingdom of God" (John 3:3). This new creature in Christ is not formed by any such method or for any such purpose as Dr. Jones' "new man."

What a perversion of the Bible's teaching and demand! How easy it is to deceive people by this "new man" vocabulary, because every Christian is vitally interested in the "new man" in Christ!

What needs to be pointed out more than anything else in regard to Dr. Jones' statements, however, is that here he defends and maintains what is called today the "inclusivist" church. This is one of the principles upon which the modern church is built. There is room in the modern church for everybody. The modernist should be included; there should be tolerance for him. Even though the creeds speak otherwise, the modernist should not be molested. He should be permitted to go on proclaiming his doctrine of the God of the Bible being a "dirty bully." It is this idea that has turned the larger churches over to the modernists. Paul says, "A little leaven leaveneth the whole lump." The failure of the Christian Church in America to discipline the unbelievers who came in as modernists accounts for their capitulation to modernism. Now the fruit of the victory of the modernists over the fundamentalists in the church is seen in the "united voice" of Protestantism telling us that we must have the social control of all economic processes for the common good!

The Church of Christ is not a hodgepodge or a forum. It is a standard. That standard must be kept unsullied and pure. It is a banner; it is a flag; it is an army marching as to war. The split that has come between the fundamentalists and the modernists has come because the fundamentalists, realizing that they could not be obedient to God and remain in fellowship with men who deny the great things of God's Word, have separated from the modernism. It is in these things that the writer believes we have hope for the blessing of God and the continuance of our liberties. Sin is real.

When it goes unjudged in the church of Jesus Christ, that body which professes to obey and honor Christ as the Head, God's favor turns from the church, and He actually gives men "strong delusions, that they should believe a lie."

Let us take a moment to say a word about Dr. Carpenter, since we reviewed his book earlier. Dr. Carpenter's emphasis is on the universal Fatherhood of God and the brotherhood of man, one of the most popular slogans of the day. In fact, Dr. Carpenter says he learned this doctrine from his mother, to whom he dedicated his book. Jesus Christ said to the religious leaders of His day, "Ye are of your father the devil, and the lusts of your father ye will do. He was a murderer from the beginning, and abode not in the truth, because there is no truth in him. When he speaketh a lie, he speaketh of his own: for he is a liar, and the father of it" (John 8:44). But these Jews had insisted that they believed in the Fatherhood of God, "We have one Father, even God." Jesus sternly replied, "If God were your Father, ye would love me: for I proceeded forth and came from God" (vs. 41, 42). Then again our Saviour declared to these same Jews, "Because I tell you the truth, ye believe me not. . . . He that is of God heareth God's words: ye therefore hear them not, because ye are not of God" (vs. 45, 47).

Jesus Christ repudiated the popular doctrine that is on the lips of thousands of preachers today—the universal Fatherhood of God. There is no such doctrine taught in the Bible. Neither does its corollary, the brotherhood of man, exist in the Bible. Countless numbers of good Christian people think that the brotherhood of man and the Fatherhood of God are the essence of the Christian faith, and it is on the wings of such words that the collectivistic idea is receiving its most favorable reception. Jesus Christ "came unto his own, and his own received him not. But as many as received him, to them gave he power to become the sons of God, even to them that believe on his name" (John 1:11, 12). The brotherhood of man and the Fatherhood of God deny the reality of sin and what sin has done in separating man from God and God from man. Sin is the greatest single factor that has wrecked their world. We must have a remedy for sin before we can have a remedy for our social problems. But when we listen to these Federal Council men calling sin what the Bible does not pronounce sin—the profit motive; when we hear them belittling and rejecting what the Bible does not pronounce sin, then we are face to face with another text of the Prophet Isaiah: "Woe unto them that call evil good, and good evil; that put darkness for light, and light for darkness; . . . which justify the wicked for reward, and take away the righteousness of the righteous from him!" (Isa. 5:20, 23.)

As a point of reflection, we cannot go on without stopping here and observing one matter. In the days of the great fundamentalist-modernist controversy inside the larger churches, back in the '30's—we remember it so well, for we were a party to it—there were, and still are, a number of fundamentalists in these denominations who refused to take part in the battle between the modernists and the fundamentalists. They said it did not matter, and refused to do battle for the honor of the Lord and the great doctrines of the faith. As a result, the battle was lost. In the Northern Baptist Convention it was lost. The liberals took over, and hundreds of Baptist churches withdrew from the Convention. In the Northern Presbyterian Church the battle was lost. The denomination split. We happened to be among the group that went out. In the Methodist Church the power and control of the bishops were such that there was very little controversy in that group; and yet, at the time of the union, groups refused to go into the union. In that great fight were not only the issues of eternity, but also the issues of our nation. The strength of those denominations taken over by the modernists is now being felt in that, through the Federal Council of the Churches of Christ in America, there is being made to us, in the full dress of the terms of the Christian religion, the offer of a philosophy that will destroy our system of private enterprise and freedom. This voice of the church has failed us. It is the failure of the church, moreover, that accounts for the rise of the tyrant. Had these churches been saved, they could not now have been used against true freedom by their social creeds!

The church of Christ has an opportunity in this day that it has never before had in all the history of its existence. Forces of communism, forces which would undercut our free democracy, are assaulting us from every hand, from without and from within. The one voice that ought to be lifted in behalf of our liberties, to explain to the nation whence these liberties came, and how they can be maintained, to warn the Government against going beyond its sphere of power and injecting itself into the sphere of the individual, and to call men to repentance and faith in the living God that men might find salvation, is the voice of the church. The true church of Christ is needed now. What an opportunity! What a challenge! What a day! The church could be the savior of the nation as it proclaims the message of the Word of God. Distressed, brokenhearted, deluded businessmen, if they heard such a message, would turn to the church and to God.

The laboring man, in his perplexity and confusion, in his strife and fear, would turn to the true church for the message of peace and liberty. The historic church has what both need. One of the ways that the modern church has had of giving currency to its solution of the problem has been to play up "sinful individualism," greed, arrogance, exploitation and then in the name of these ills, which are present in more or less degree in the capitalistic order, to ask that the order of free enterprise be abandoned. Thus men have looked at the evils without careful thought and have been ready to accept the solution of a planned economy.

It is here that we can see, in its finest delineations, the contrast between the collectivistic idea of power and the Christian concept of liberty. The historic Christian church recognizes the sin of greed, of selfishness, and of exploitation; but it does not ask us to abandon the system of the profit motive as bad, for to do so would punish not only the greedy and the exploiters, but also all those who legitimately use the profit motive.

The true church asks two things: first, that the state use its power to punish evildoers,—as our creeds dealing with the power of the magistrates indicate; and second, that the church use its message of salvation, the power of God, to change the individual!

The system of planned economy says that we shall have brotherhood and equality—an enforced brotherhood, an enforced equality—brought about by the very order of society itself. Through the power of the State, men are compelled to give up the profit motive. They are forbidden, by the rules of the order, to exercise the profit motive. The State is their Master. The State's power was never intended for such a purpose!

In free economy there is an additional factor, the most important factor of all, the very highest pinnacle to which we can go in this study; and as we come to it now we do so with the very greatest of joy.

The Ten Commandments, which give us the system of

private enterprise, were handed down to Moses by God. It is the violation of those commandments which makes sin. "Sin is the transgression of the law." When men in greediness, in exploitation, and in deceitfulness get their gain, they are not sinning against society only; they are sinning primarily against the eternal and living God. Society cannot adequately judge them though it may pass laws and condemn them, which it does; but the ultimate and the eternal Judge is God, and He must be heard. The point is that the acts of man in relation to these commandments are to be judged by God not merely in this world but in that which is to come.

Dr. Oxnam does not like such a terrible God. But the true God is a God of infinite justice, of infinite wrath, and He has ordained His church to stand upon this earth and proclaim His law, to hold the law of God up to men on every hand, to show them that they are sinners, that they are condemned. The moral law, in other words, which maintains this free order for free men, is an eternal law; a society established upon the Ten Commandments and preserving the rights of the individual in a free society, as demanded by those commandments, is a society upon which the favor of God will abound. "Righteousness exalteth a nation, but sin is a reproach to any people."

Let us proceed. Man, the capitalist in a free economy, has a soul. He also dies. His breath is in his nostrils; he is here today and gone tomorrow. He must face his Maker; he must stand before the judgment bar of God and render an account for his deeds done in the flesh. If he is guilty of sin, how shall he stand in the presence of a holy God? By the law comes the knowledge of sin. Paul said, "I had not known sin except the law had said, Thou shalt not covet." The one thing that the church of Christ needs to hold up before men and to preach is the great law of God. Oh, yes, the modern church talks about the moral law, but it is the moral law in which all men are brothers and God is the Father of everybody, the moral law of their own imagining, not the moral law of the eternal God which demands free creatures, free to obey His law.

If the law applies to the laboring man, his hatred of the capitalist is seen. His bitterness and strife against those who have gain and who make the profit are condemned. The law hits labor and capitalist alike. The law condemns both. Here it is that we have come into the very presence of the greatest message of all time. Sinners are condemned by the law, bound to face the eternal God, without hope; but the God, who gave the law at Sinai, gave us His Son at Calvary to make an atonement for that sin and to provide reconciliation. So it is that the church preaches the Gospel of Christ. "Christ died for our sins according to the scriptures" (1 Cor. 15:3). To a man who has heard the law and has seen his own sin condemned before it, that message is good news. It is the greatest news the world has ever heard. There is deliverance. There is salvation. A man can stand in the presence of his Maker and sing, "I am redeemed"—saved by faith and by faith alone. "The fear of the Lord [not the fear of the State] is the beginning of wisdom."

It is this message that begets love, love for God and love for fellow men; it is only here that "love shines in." The strife between capital and labor and the tyranny that comes down upon men in a collectivistic state do not generate love. They produce hate. It is only the grace of God that begets love, and that is what we need. It can come only through the preaching of the Gospel. It was this Gospel that gave us our land. It was the law of God, believed in the hearts of men who feared Him, that gave us our Constitution. It was that same faith that wrote into the great creeds of Christendom the rights of the individual, made these rights paramount, and guaranteed security in freedom of enterprise.

Patrick Henry gives us a statement that goes to the heart of this matter:

> "Bad men cannot make good citizens. It is impossible that a nation of infidels or idolaters should be a nation of free men. It is when a people forget God that tyrants forge their chains. A vitiated state of morals, a corrupted public conscience, are incompatible with freedom.
>
> "No free government, or the blessings of liberty can be preserved to any people but by a firm adherence to justice, moderation, temperance, frugality, and virtue, and by a frequent recurrence to fundamental principles."

What is actually happening, so far as the Federal Council is concerned, is that when it sees exploitation and similar sins of society, it turns to the State to remove this condition by controlling the whole of society, instead of emphasizing more vigorously the preaching of the Gospel and the fundamental principles of society. What society needs is not the State to control it, but a more vigorous presentation of the Gospel of the grace of God. Society needs to have the Bible presented to it. The modern church, forsaking its own task, is asking the nation to do for society by force what the church should do for society in the free exercise of religion. The one is tyranny; the other, freedom.

Yes, the modern church turns to the authoritarian state for the control of the individual. The final problem we face is not that we socially control the individual, but that the individual be changed, his heart changed. It is not our free economy that needs "redemption" or change; it is the individual in it that must be redeemed; and this is possible only in Jesus Christ. The Gospel of the grace of God alone frees men. We do not want the power of the State to change men—it cannot do it. Such a hope is vain. We want the power of God—this alone reaches the soul. This power and wisdom are manifested in the Gospel of Jesus Christ.

Oh, Church, why not preach only this Christ? The Apostle Paul said, "I determined not to know any thing among you, save Jesus Christ, and him crucified" (1 Cor. 2:2). Where is that emphasis in the church today?

Oh, Church, why not give the only message that can change men, and be done with the substitute of totalitarianism? Throw away your "social Gospel" and give us the historic Christ!

Oh, Church, why, O why, are you spending your time and energy for what is not bread, but in truth a serpent?

Yes, this is one reason for tyranny.

The historic Christian church looks beyond time into eternity to the individual's presence before the living God. The appeal of the modern church is only to time, and gives us communism with its tyranny. The appeal of the historic Christian church gave us Western civilization with its liberty. It was this appeal, and this appeal alone, that gave us America. "By the fear of the Lord men depart from evil."

As the message of the Gospel in its fullness comes home to free men in a free order, it tells them that God commands their time and their money. In fact, God's Word asks for one-tenth of all our money. "Will a man rob God? Yet ye have robbed me. But ye say, Wherein have we robbed thee? In tithes and offerings" (Mal. 3:8). Think what ten per cent of the national income is! If the gains made by our free enterprise in America were tithed, we should have all the money needed for hospitals, for the needy, for the poor, for the unemployed. If ten per cent of all the money that the capitalists in the United States make were turned over to the cause of Christ in this country, it would be used for the preservation of liberty. Just think how it could be used for preaching the Gospel today with our attractive means of reaching people! The church preaches stewardship; it preaches benevolence; it preaches everything that we saw in the section of this book dealing with the Word of God. This is what God wants men to do.

When we were delivering the series of messages out of which this particular thesis came, we received a letter from a lady in the radio congregation asking for a copy of the message in order that she could give it to her brother who is not a Christian, but who saw the error in the communistic setup. She said that if her brother could read these messages she felt he would be more interested in the message of redemption and might become a Christian. That dear woman is absolutely right. It is the approach and the appeal that we have made in this book that will turn men to Christ, for in Him alone is liberty. We shall always love liberty when we love Christ.

We are suffering today from the famine of the Word in the land. Many of our churches are empty; on Sunday night thousands of them are closed; our people are indifferent. The world has moved in and claimed the church as its respectable clubhouse. Secularism has killed the Spirit of God, and the passion of the would-be servants of Christ has grown cold. All of this and more can be traced directly to the rejection of the Word of God by these leaders of His church. All of this and more is the reason for tyranny.

When He who is the Light of the world is pushed out of His church and men use His name to designate another christ, when there is not another, the Light has gone out; and when men use the words of His historic church to connote another idea from what He gave them, the salt truly has lost its savor and men trample it under foot. We must come back to the Bible; believe it, preach it, obey it. It is all that we have.

The sudden passing of the late President Roosevelt revealed a depth of spiritual content in the nation's life that we have never seen before. For three days the radios cancelled all commercials and gave us hymns, religious services, Scripture passages, eulogies. We never before, in so short a time, heard so much Gospel on the air. The heart of America was moved. We remember especially the broadcast that came from Charlotte, North Carolina, as the funeral train passed through on its way to Washington. Thirty-five thousand people, we were told, gathered to pay final tribute. Flowers were put over the railroad tracks; and the people sang. We heard them singing. What did they sing? "The Church's One Foundation," "Onward, Christian Soldiers," "The Old Rugged Cross." They were Gospel hymns of the way of salvation. Yes, it is all that we have.

President Truman's first address to the assembled Houses of Congress had more reference to divine help than any other presidential message in the memory of this writer. He had in his heart, he said, the prayer of Solomon. He asked God for wisdom, and he closed that message by saying that he wanted only to be a faithful servant of his Lord and of his people. How we thrilled when we heard that!

Yes, it is all that we have—the Bible. Yet these modern churchmen do not believe it. They say it has error in it; the God who gave it to the prophets lied; He was a "dirty bully." These men have rejected its authority and have taken refuge in some other authority— what they call the living church, the church that has gone away from the precepts of the Scriptures and the liberties which they demand, or the authority that is "within them." "If therefore the light that is in thee be darkness, how great is that darkness!" (Matt. 6:23.) This is the reason for tyranny.

Since what we speak of as the modern church, expressing itself through the Federal Council of the Churches of Christ in America, is not giving us this message, but is actually aiding and abetting the whole communistic propaganda throughout the world, the responsibility resting upon the churches that are true to the Gospel is infinitely increased. How shall we fulfill that responsibility and what shall we do for the preservation of our liberties? It is the answer to this question that we shall endeavor to give in our final chapter.

CHAPTER 14

THE BATTLE FOR FREEDOM

"THE Battle for Freedom" is the appropriate name for our closing chapter. We could call it "The Battle for America," for that is what is involved.

Shall we sit idly by and let these modern churchmen lead us as a nation into controlled social economy as their glorified "kingdom of God"? Or shall we resist their campaign? The answer of every liberty-loving American should be "Resist!" To do so involves controversy, fighting. Not to do so might give us temporary ease and peace but tyranny and death for certain in the end.

One of the attitudes that the modern church leaders have been successful in imparting to Christian people generally is the notion that it is wrong for Christians to enter into controversy, and that for a Christian minister to do so manifests a bad spirit and an un-Christlike attitude. This false notion of tolerance—pacifism (for such it is) within the church—explains one reason why the modern churchmen have been able to capture the larger denominations for their radical propaganda. And, if we dare to listen to it any longer, it will also account for the loss of our freedom in America.

In the most subtle, most unsuspecting manner, in the most disarming place imaginable, America is having poured into her ears Sunday after Sunday, in pulpit after pulpit, on radio after radio, as the Federal Council leaders speak, ideas that are essentially collectivistic. If this were being done under cover, or in the dark, we might be suspicious; but when it is being done in broad daylight we think little about it. The voice of the church is being used to impress the leaders of the nation, the representatives of the people in Congress, to do certain things in the name of democracy; and the conflict is on in Washington. The battle between the two different ideologies is a battle of which every Congressman is keenly conscious—more so today than perhaps at any other time. The subhead on a news story appearing in the press was the statement of a United States Senator of a Government bureaucrat, "He thinks it is sin to make a profit."

A fight as serious and as desperate as any waged in World War II is going on. It is a life-or-death struggle, and everyone of us must get into it quickly, or it will destroy our freedom and our children.

If the idea presented to us, as we have seen it in this study, if the voice of the modern church prevails in the minds of men in America, especially in the minds of the young men coming to power and influence in our land, our American way of life will become the way of the tyrant. Of course it will still be called our "good old American democracy." The battle must be joined wherever the enemy is found! Surely, we can use the word "enemy" now without being accused of being unkind. Have we not seen that the position of the modern church is diametrically opposed; first, to that of the Bible; second, to that of the historic creeds; third, to that of the Bill of Rights? Surely any organization in this country whose propaganda cuts the very foundation from under these structural columns of our society is an enemy.

The question is, Will this collectivistic idea of a controlled economy win America, or shall we keep her free?

Because of the religious nature of the conflict,—ideas being offered in the name of the church and on the authority of the Gospel of Jesus Christ, falsely so-called,—this issue partakes of all the aggravated complications of the conflict of the ages: tyranny versus freedom, darkness versus light, error versus truth, Satan versus Christ. This is the battle line. It all fits into the picture that we have seen. The attack upon the Old Testament, the rejecting of the creeds, the assault upon the miracles, the rise of the evolutionary theory form the cannonade that we have been hearing in generations past and which has been tearing down the citadel of freedom. The battle has reached such a proportion and has come to such a stage that the enemy now comes forth with his clearcut attempt to take over not only the society but also the man, the individual man who has occupied this citadel and shared the blessings of liberty that God's Word has given to civilization. It has been a long, hard struggle. Our forefathers fought in this conflict in its various stages, and now the battle for freedom seems to fall upon us as one mammoth avalanche. What shall we do?

We must not underestimate the strength and the nature of our enemy. This was a common failing in dealing with the nazi and fascist types of totalitarian power. The powers that represent the ideology we have analyzed and exposed in this study may be placed in three pronounced groups: first, Russia; second, radical movements within the United States, including radical labor; third, the Federal Council of the Churches of Christ in America, which we have so thoroughly studied and exposed here. A brief word about each needs to be said in this summary.

First, Russia. In the present world conflagration nazism has been destroyed. This particular tyranny has gone from the earth—at least for a while. But Russia has risen to a place of world dominance. Her influence is beginning to dominate not only all Europe, but also Asia, from the Atlantic to the Pacific. To deny this would be folly. In a real sense Russia has become the Number 1 nation of the world. She is strong. Her regimentation has given her a type of strength that may assert itself. On the other hand, we, of course, believe that the democracies have strength, and that, in their notion of liberty, there is far greater power than there is in controlled economy. Such is true. It is only because of the strength left in the democracies that Hitler has been crushed as he has. But Russia has an ally for her ideology inside the United States, not in some underground force, but in the most respected institution the nation has, the voice of the church.

The conflict, which the world recognizes, between the Russian ideology and the American ideology is not a conflict between the continents only. So far as the ideology is concerned, there is little or no conflict inside Russia. Her iron hand sees to that. But it is in the Western world, the "free democratic world," particularly the United States, that this conflict is now raging. If America can be strong in her independence and liberty, if America can be thoroughly established in her private enterprise system, she will be in a place of tremendous leadership and power. Russia could never conquer her. But America, at this very moment, is facing crisis after crisis in which the modern church, Russia's most powerful ideological ally, is pushing its way into our state chambers and clamoring for power and expression in our social life. Unwittingly, we have been led by the voice of the church to believe that many of the Russian ideas are sound and in accord with our American heritage. As a result we are being weakened. There is confusion. Russia does not need a communist party in the United States when she has such an ally in the leadership furnished by Protestant churches in the Federal Council and in such leaders as Harry F. Ward, G. Bromley Oxnam, E. Stanley Jones, James Myers, and J. Henry Carpenter. To say that the matter is serious is putting it mildly.

To say that we have the Word of God on our side, that the position of the historic Christian church supports our line of battle, and that the Bill of Rights in the Constitution of the United States is our bulwark means very little when the great mass of the people is being led away from these things by the subtle phrases and propaganda of the hour. These institutions of freedom are at the mercy of the people. Constitutional guarantees and restraints mean little at the hands of a deceived public. During the days of war, America bled for freedom, but what we need now more than anything else is a true understanding of what liberty is. What is called liberty in the Russian concept is not liberty at all. What is called democracy in the Russian terminology is not democracy at all. It is in the confusion of these terms that men are being misled and the battle is being so difficult to wage. The finest illustration of this was the address of Molotov at San Francisco. He spoke of the Russian system as "democratic" in the "true" sense of the word.

Do not think, however, that Russia is being misled or confused. She sees the distinction clearly and is concerned about the countries around her. It seems increasingly apparent that Russia wants more than merely to dominate Europe and Asia, so far as her influence is concerned. She wants Europe and Asia to become communistic.

On April 22, 1945, in a dispatch from Moscow by C. L. Sulzberger, published in the Philadelphia *Record* of April 23rd, this very question is raised by Moscow. Mr. Sulzberger writes:

"An effort to insist that democracy in Europe should be constructed exactly like the British or American models would represent an unjustified effort to interfere in the internal affairs of other peoples, A. Sokoloff said yesterday in *War and the Working Class*.

"Sokoloff's views and prognostications on international affairs are often surprisingly accurate. He said:

" 'Indisputably there is a difference between the democracy that is fulfilled in the Soviet and the democracy that is applied in a number of other countries. . . .

" 'It would be a completely hopeless business to demand that democracy in all European countries should be built exactly on the lines of the English or American example.' "

The Russian paper then continues to assert that such a claim would constitute a disruptive influence in the internal affairs of other people. In other words, the American idea of democracy, the American concept of freedom, and the liberation of conquered countries for which America has been fighting, with a view to making them free, would in the attitude of this Russian authority "constitute an attempt to disturb the internal affairs of other peoples that could not be justified by anything: An attempt to force on them from outside certain political canons." We thought they wanted our concept of freedom? For what have we been liberating them? So that they could become communistic and later fight us?

The article further describes the nature of Russian democracy in favorable terms, and—by the way—in terms that are very similar to those we have seen in the Federal Council's documents, while, at the same time, taking a slap at the British and American concept.

"The economic regime in the Soviet guarantees to the citizens of our country the possibility of realizing their democratic rights, among which are such vital rights as the rights of labor, education and freedom from exploitation or racial or national inequality. One should not forget that in England only the metropolitan population has democratic rights, while the much more numerous population of the British colonies still expects democratization in vain, as well as freedom and independence."

Surely in this we have an evidence that Russia wants the democratic countries about her to be dominated by her political canons. And in the light of this, so far as Europe is concerned, it appears more and more true that America has been liberating Europe to make it free for communism. Russia is on the march in more ways than one.

Since it is clearly the Russian ideology that we have been examining in this thesis, at this point we must say a word or two about Russia's present place. We have indicated that we believe she wants to rule Europe and Asia, but how about her relationship in the international sphere in the security organization the United Nations set up at San Francisco? The one question that stands out is "Can Russia be trusted?" The one emphasis of the leaders of the United Nations, in going to the San Francisco Conference, was that there had to be mutual trust. At the very moment they were uttering these words, Russia, in her handling of the Polish question, was giving the world an example of lack of faith. At Yalta, Roosevelt and Churchill compromised with Stalin on the Polish question, giving a part of Poland to Russia. Russia signed the agreement that recognized that, until the people of Poland, by free elections, could establish their own government, Poland should have a temporary government, representative of all parties. Stalin signed this. The taking of Polish territory and giving it to the Russians did not satisfy the world, but we were told that we have to compromise and that the world can go on only by a series of compromises. We must now be "realists." But when our boys were encouraged to fight and die we were "idealists," believers in the four freedoms. What a change in emphasis! But let us go on.

Roosevelt died; Stalin immediately signed an agreement with the Lublin Government, the Soviet-sponsored (Communist) Polish Government, and demanded that this government be seated at the San Francisco Conference. This precipitated a crisis that shook the United States and cast a shadow over the San Francisco meeting. The question remained a deadlock and the conference attempted to side step the issue. Stalin had not stood by the Yalta agreement. Again we were told that there would have to be a compromise of some kind so that the solution could be worked out! Stalin apparently has learned that the way to get gains is to make demands, and then, with a compromise, gain a portion of what he wants. By the pursuing of such political conduct, over a period of time he will be able really to get somewhere in international affairs.

There is another angle to this, however, that is significant. Russia largely fought her own war until the Teheran Conference in 1944. Remember, it was Hitler who compelled the United States to be an ally of Russia. At first there was no collaboration with the United Nations or with the supreme command of the Allied forces; and during that time, through lend-lease, we were giving Russia millions of dollars' worth of goods free. In fact, it has been reported that almost everything on wheels in Russia is American-made. The way we have helped Russia win the war has strengthened her to such an extent that she is now able to defy us and the world; and there seems to be little doubt but what that is exactly what Russia intends to do.

The tragedy, so far as the United States is concerned, is not only that we have weakened ourselves but also that, in taking a strong stand against the totalitarianism of Hitler in the demands of an unconditional surrender, we have failed to protect ourselves from the attack of an equally disastrous totalitarianism and a more subtle form of tyranny. We are faced in our attitude toward Russian communism with the same perils and temptations that the world faced in its dealings with Hitler as he came to power. Right now the world so desperately wants lasting peace, it so passionately wants bloodshed to be stopped, that we are ready to make almost any sacrifice to bring it to pass, even if the sacrifice involves "compromises" that are in reality a subtle destruction of our American freedom. It is the same old story of appeasement.

Chamberlain came home from Munich with his umbrella in his hand and announced a "peace in our time," but he had slaughtered Czechoslovakia. We went to a United Nations Conference in San Francisco and declared, "Peace forever," but we have, in the name of compromise, slaughtered Poland and appeased Russia. There is absolutely no difference in the two positions so far as principle or fact is concerned. From the first meeting of Roosevelt with Stalin we have been soft and apparently afraid. We have done all the conceding and the backing down. The war against totalitarianism is not ended with Germany. Hitler himself conducted his conquest in the name of liberation and freedom. Stalin has used the same words with us—freedom and independence—and American resistance has been worn down to the Russian ideology because we have rejoiced in her victories over Germany. America is coming out of the war with her resistance to the Russian ideology weakened, with her treasury depleted. America has been the good old "grandfather" to the world. We fought a war for freedom, and we have come out of it desperately in debt, internally divided over the Russian ideology, confused about the nature of freedom, with thousands upon thousands of our boys dead and maimed, and with Russia defying us and telling us not to give to the nations that we have liberated in Europe the kind of freedom we have known in America. Some war! It is not that we should not have helped, but it is the way we have done it that is wrong. Has this Second World War been fought to make the world safe for communism? What will be the verdict of history?

We have not won the war for freedom just because Hitler is dead. The battle against totalitarianism and in behalf of freedom is a much larger and broader war than that against nazism and fascism. It is this restricted, narrow view that has hurt and crippled America. Russia must be dealt with, if she cannot be trusted—and we believe she cannot be, for her morality and ethics are diametrically opposed to those of the free democracies.

Anne O'Hare McCormick, writing from San Francisco, during the security conference, May 6, had this to say about the Russian and American systems:

"The two systems start from different premises and use the same words in different meanings. It is supremely difficult to translate one into the other. All the headaches of this convention center in the relationship between the Soviet Union and the other United Nations. Essentially they boil down to the interrelationship of the Soviet Union and the United States. If these two powers cannot enter

into a partnership for peace, the machinery being blue-
printed here will never safeguard the peace."

You cannot translate the one into the other—the ideologies
are irreconcilable because of their "different premises." This
is simply the truth as this entire study from the Bible proves.

The only language that Russia knows is the language of
force. She will take all or as much of the world as she thinks
she can, and she has already started that march in her dealings in Poland and in her demands that our ideas of democracy should not be foisted upon the European countries that,
in the name of freedom, have been delivered.

The real battle for freedom just began when VE-Day was
announced. It is not easy to write these words. These are
hard facts to face, but we shall have to face them if we love
liberty.

At whatever cost, we must not lose sight of liberty. The
San Francisco conference, in its emphasis upon the securing
of the peace which the world so passionately wants, has one
big underlying question, "Is the peace going to be a peace,
with liberty?" We have fought the war for liberty, and we
must fight the peace for liberty. The emphasis of the peace
has all been upon "lasting peace" not upon "peace for liberty." If it were the latter emphasis, there would be more
occasion for dispute with Russia over "freedom." So there
we are again. This is why the drive for an "International
Bill of Rights" is stymied, too. How could Russia grant
freedom of the press?

If the peace structure set up involves compromise with the
principles of liberty—our American concept of freedom—the
United States should not go into it. This is going to be the
greatest temptation and the most subtle deception involved
in the whole program. In other words, if the international

organization is to provide for the continual advance of communism throughout the world because of its compromise with the fundamental principles of liberty, then we have lost the peace—and lost America.

The opening of the conference had a bad sound. It was compromise, compromise, compromise. Yes, there must be practical compromises—none of us could live without them—but there can be no compromise with the principles of liberty. It is on liberty that the world organization must be established—not the Russian idea of liberty, but the American idea. There can be no compromise between the two. To compromise is to embrace the Russian concept. Surely, in our previous chapters, we have seen the logic and the truth of this in our analysis of the Federal Council leaders' works, and this logic and truth apply with the same force to the world security organization. If Russia is willing to work along in a world security organization where the fundamental principles of liberty are maintained, well and good; but it is exceedingly doubtful whether Russia has any such intention. In view of these facts, it is essential that the United States and Great Britain, the English-speaking democracies, maintain their strength. We must have post-war military conscription. Yet, the one emphasis of the churches, after VJ-Day will be "disarm," and this will further strengthen Russia and her ideology.

In the truest possible sense, private enterprise has won this war. It was the American assembly line, our industrial power, that made possible the winning of the Second World War; and yet it is the ideology of collectivism that would destroy this enterprise and that is now tempting, confusing, and terrorizing the world. Are we to build Russia's industrial system to where it can outrank ours, and give her the balance of power? If so, the logical and irreconcilable conflict between the two ideologies will burst forth into a mammoth world conflict in another twenty-five years or less. In the strength that is ours at the present moment we must stand uncompromisingly by the principles of liberty, even if it means that we must refuse to go into the international organization where these principles are compromised, if such be the case. The post-war period, from every possible angle, is going to be far more critical, so far as the United States is concerned, than any of the crises of the war.

When, within our own borders, we look at the picture we have described in this story, it is indeed desperate and disheartening. What has the Second World War done for us—not for us as a nation but for the idea of freedom that we cherish and under which alone men can be men, and for which we supposedly fought the war?

Second, Radical Labor. It is not our purpose here to discuss all radical organizations. We mentioned the radical labor issues because the Federal Council raised them by its actions and propaganda. Radical labor is one of the most aggressive and most potent forces seeking to change our social order. I have a splendid illustration.

While I was in the midst of writing this analysis, I received, unsolicited, through the mail a large envelope from the Communist Political Association of Camden County, the county in which I live. There were two pieces of literature enclosed.

The first was an attractive folder appealing to me for my personal subscription for the support of the communist committee's work. I was given a detailed statement as to just how the funds were to be used. They were to be used for the propagation of the "Marxist principles" and "democratic ideals," the two supposedly being synonymous.

The second piece of literature was a thirty-one-page

speech by Earl Browder. On the front is a picture of an angry-looking Uncle Sam, rolling up his sleeves. The title is "America's Decisive Battle." The pamphlet contains the "text of a report by Earl Browder, President of the Communist Political Association, to a meeting of its National Committee, held in New York City, March 10, 1945." The last two sections of the address are entitled "Position of the Communist Political Association" and "International Aspects of Marxism."

Under the first we read:

"We are holding the first meeting of our National Committee since the founding of our Association last May, following the dissolution of the Communist Party. It is in order, therefore, to make something of a summary analysis of where our organization stands as a result of the tremendous world events and of the changes in our own organization."

Then follows a list of the gains made which include:

"Our basic judgments on the political currents of our country and the world have been confirmed by events. . . .

"Our political influence within the labor and progressive organizations and communities has grown far wider and deeper than it ever was before.

"Our own organization is more unified than ever, it grows, and it carries on more work in a more efficient manner with more results.

"We are gradually breaking down and dissolving the barriers built up against us over a generation by the dominant forces in American society. . . .

"All of our success flows from the fact that over the years we had equipped ourselves with the highest of sciences, Marxism, the science of history which enables us not only to understand events but to help shape them; because we understood that Marxism is not a dogma but a guide to action in the present unique historical moment. . . .

"We are linking ourselves indissolubly with ever-widening masses of people. From all this arises our confidence.

"We will continue to go forward unhesitatingly upon our chosen path."

The concluding section of the booklet, "International Aspects of Marxism," is so pertinent to this entire thesis that we give it in full:

"American Communists have not been affiliated with any international organization since November 1940. We are not now, except that as Americans we are affiliated with the rapidly crystallizing United Nations organization, and as trade unionists we share in the rising World Trade Union Federation. But we always were and remain internationalists in spirit and understanding. We therefore retain the deepest interest in the life and progress of Marxists in other lands, as a part of our general interest in the whole world. There is an inevitable kinship and identity between Marxists of all lands, as between men and women who work with similar tools for similar ends with similar results. It is not the product merely of organization, and therefore it is not abolished when organizational connections no longer exist.

"As to the Marxists leading the Soviet Union, the whole world now knows that it is indebted to them for being rescued from an age of reversion to cannibalism, to which Hitler had dragged most of Europe. They have long been the high inspiration of Marxists everywhere. Now they are an equal inspiration to all democratic peoples of the world. Marxists of all lands aspire to serve their own countries with something of the effectiveness displayed by the Marxists of the Soviet Union under the leadership of the greatest Marxist, Stalin.

"America is now awakening to the fact that the Marxists, the Communists, of China are in the forefront of our great struggle against the Japanese, that they are most loyal and dependable allies—even though for years the dominant American attitude had been to consider them enemies or at least definitely 'undesirable.' Today it is official U. S. policy to urge the full inclusion of the Chinese Communists into the Chinese government, because this is necessary to achieve a strong China and U. S. interests demand a strong China.

"Everywhere in Latin America the Marxists are actively in the forefront of the rising labor and democratic movements, and becoming a major political force. The outstanding and unchallenged leader of the Latin American Federation of Labor is Vicente Lombardo Toledano, who, although he has never been affiliated with any Communist Party, is a talented and self-proclaimed Marxist.

"In Europe the people of every country liberated from the Axis have put forward the Marxists among their most trusted leaders; no government in such liberated countries can make the slightest claim to stability unless it includes the Communists.

"Marxism is the only school of political thought which is emerging from this greatest of all wars with strength not only unimpaired but increased manifold.

"It is the high mission of the Communist Political Association to prove that Americans do not lag far behind this great historical trend, to worthily represent in our own country this science, Marxism, which is as universal as the knowledge of astronomy, as practical as radar, as international as human culture and progress."

What better possible evidence could we produce than this of the aggressive, brilliant manner in which the Marxist philosophy is being propagated. Read again what Mr. Browder says about Marxism's emerging from this war. They are able to get the crowds out to their rallies. They are holding classes and schools. They are circularizing other preachers just as they circularized me. Is it that they believe the ministry is a fertile field for their sympathies? They are just as much aware as we are of the condition we have exposed in this volume, and all of this Earl Browder calls "America's Decisive Battle." The last of May, 1945, Earl Browder recognized a rebuke of his policies of collaborating with the capitalists, given by the French Communist. He indicated that there may be a change in policy following the war, and a return to the Communist Party and the class warfare. Whichever procedure is used, either the Communist Political Association or the Communist Party, the aims and activities of Earl Browder and his fellow travelers in the United States remain the same. This is the battle that the world will witness in the post-war era.

Third, the Federal Council. Let us go back now to the strongest ally of Russia and the radical labor movement, within the United States,—the Federal Council. To tell men that the message of the present-day church in the United States cannot be trusted when it holds before them this planned economy and attacks the profit motive is almost like telling a man that his mother is deceiving him. People simply will not believe when told that the modern church is leading us away from our American heritage. To fight this battle at the present stage of developments is to fight from the most unenviable position. The enemy has been carrying on this battle for a long time; he has endeavored to maneuver the circumstances so that the opposition will be at a disadvantage. But this does not mean for one moment that we despair, but rather that we shall intensify our efforts, hoist the flag, and march to battle.

It is a battle. Do you think for one moment that the Federal Council leaders are going to give up the words "liberty" and "democracy" as they have been using them? Of course not. They will fight to keep them with the meanings Marx gave them! Do you think for one moment that they will sit idly by and accept the charge that they are advocating a system that would destroy our American freedom and undermine the Constitution of the United States? Of course not. They will deny it vigorously. They will, and even do at the present, declare that they do not want to be like Russia. They may be, as we have demonstrated, advocating the Russian idea in its germ and kernel, but in their society, a society patterned after that idea, they want also to inject into it the God element. But this does not alter the charge one iota. The facts, the logic, the application of their ideas, and the implications of their position—for which they have been willing to go all out in the name of Christ—place them exactly where we have put them in this discussion, and they must be held to it. Do you think for one minute that they would be insane enough to admit that they are trying to take our liberties from us? No, they are the ones who tell us that Russia is really "changing" from her radical extremes. No, they are the ones who will attempt to smear those who lift their voices against these Russian "ideas" coming to power in the United States of America. No, they will accuse anyone who exposes their Marxist ideology, as attempting to sabotage international collaboration, by creating ill will against Russia,—or some similar line. Those who fight for our American ideals of democracy, within our own America, as opposed to the Federal Council's, will be accused of belittling what Russia did as an ally, or of opposing or jeopardizing world peace. But such strategy and falsehoods must not deter us.

Let us go back to Dr. Carpenter's idea of the battle. These men all realize that they are advocating a position that is revolutionary and involves controversy, but they would like to put their ideas across without the controversy, if possible. Dr. Carpenter put it this way:

"For religion to supply one motive [the motive of cooperation which he is advocating], and the economic world another which stands in direct and irreconcilable contradiction to it, is to breed a conflict whose first result is psychological distress, whose ultimate effect is the ruin of both the individual and organized society" (p. 11).

To state this in the terms of the present conflict: for religion to provide one motive, and for the historic church and the Constitution of the United States and the Word of God to provide another, means that the battle line drawn for the ruin of the individual in organized society is right here.

As to where each liberty-loving American should stand and will stand in this issue as soon as he is fully informed, there can be no doubt. He will stand with the forces that are organizing for the defense of freedom in the homeland against even the modern church.

This is the place to indicate how effectively the Federal Council is carrying on its battle and the way in which it musters and uses its strength. On June 7, 1944, Dr. Samuel

McCrea Cavert, general secretary of the Federal Council, appeared before the Committee on Labor of the House of Representatives of the Seventy-eighth Congress, second session, on behalf of Bill H.R. 3986, H.R. 4004, and H.R. 4005. These bills all had to do with the general subject of prohibiting discrimination in employment. Dr. Cavert declared:

"I speak in favor of the proposed legislation on this subject, as a representative of the Protestant churches co-operating in the Federal Council."

In opening his testimony he had this to say:

"Madam Chairman, my name is Samuel McCrea Cavert. I am general secretary of the Federal Council of the Churches of Christ in America and appear to express its views, as stated in official action of its executive committee.

"The Federal Council of the Churches of Christ in America is a federation of 25 national denominations, with a membership in excess of 25,000,000, in 150,000 local congregations in all parts of the Nation."

In enlarging upon the strength of his position in representing the Protestant churches Dr. Cavert said:

"The council, as a whole, meets biennially in plenary session, made up of approximately 450 official delegates appointed by the 25 denominations in proportion to their numerical strength. In the interim, between the biennial meetings, an executive committee meets bimonthly. It is made up of approximately 90 members also representing the 25 denominations. Each denomination, whether large or small, has 2 members, and the larger ones have a proportionately greater number of representatives."

Thus we have an illustration of the way the Federal Council operates in Washington to bring pressure to bear upon the Government for the advancement of its view. Invariably, it has stood on the side of collectivism. The very bill in behalf of which Dr. Cavert appeared before Congress was designed to compel private enterprise, under the force of the Government, not to do what it—the Federal Council—considered to be discrimination in employment. The whole spirit of this legislation is contrary to the teaching of American freedom and is, in itself, an attack upon the free economy of our private enterprise system. *

Who are these 25 million people who are here being put on record in the Federal Council's activity against private enterprise? This is the place to list the denominations that are in the Federal Council so that our readers may see for themselves whether they are or are not actually members of the Federal Council and a part of this attack against our private enterprise system. Undoubtedly, the revelation of the fact will come as a real shock to many of our readers. Instead of being lined up against this attack upon our freedom as we have seen it in this story, as unquestionably many of our readers will be at this point, they will be solemnly informed that they are a part of this very system that they so honestly oppose. If your denomination is one of those mentioned, if your local church is a member of one of the denominations mentioned, then you are one of the 25 million individuals for whom the Federal Council claims to speak, and your church is one of the 150,000 individual churches which the Federal Council represents. Surely this brings the issue right home to each one of us, not only in our own town, or our own home, but in our own individual life.

The denominations in the Federal Council are as follows: Northern Baptist Convention, National Baptist Convention,

Church of the Brethren, Congregational Christian Churches, Disciples of Christ, African Methodist Episcopal Zion Church, Colored Methodist Episcopal Church in America, Moravian Church, Presbyterian Church in the U.S.A., Presbyterian Church in the U.S. (South), Protestant Episcopal Church, Reformed Church in America, Evangelical Church, Evangelical and Reformed Church, Friends, Methodist Church, African Methodist Episcopal Church, Seventh Day Baptist Churches, Ukrainian Orthodox Church of America, United Brethren Church, United Church of Canada, United Lutheran Church of America (Consultative), United Presbyterian Church, Russian Orthodox Church.

The Reformed Episcopal Church, on May 24, 1945, withdrew from the Federal Council by a vote of 66 to 33. This action was taken in its biennial meeting held in Philadelphia. The decision was made on a clear-cut doctrinal issue. The church withdrew because it believed that the Federal Council was no longer loyal to the Word of God and the historic Protestant faith.

This means that there are only twenty-four denominations comprising the Federal Council, and that other references to twenty-five denominations appearing in this book need to be considered in the light of this action of the Reformed Episcopal Church.

This action on the part of this denomination represents a major victory for the forces of evangelicalism in the United States. It is the first denomination to withdraw from the Federal Council on the doctrinal issues which have been raised in recent years.

An illustration of the way in which the Federal Council promotes itself and the cause of radicalism was furnished us in the broadcast, "Religion in the News," for April 7, 1945, by Walter W. Van Kirk. Dr. Van Kirk is a radical pacifist and secretary of the Federal Council's Commission on a Just and Durable Peace. Every Saturday night, in the name of the Federal Council, he receives fifteen minutes of free time on N.B.C. for the presentation of what news he thinks significant. On this particular date he called attention to the charter that had recently been drafted and issued in the name of Eric Johnson, Philip Murray, and William Green—a charter for labor and capital. One of the points recognized in this was the right of collective bargaining. Dr. Van Kirk took this expression and called attention to the Social Creed of the church, and declared that the church had led the way in this social development. He actually claimed credit for the advance, and used it to promote the church as a far-seeing, progressive institution in the social field. He did not tell us, however, that Plank 1 and Plank 2 of the Social Creed he was commending to the nation because of its one collective bargaining plank has in it the vicious and disastrous collectivism so foreign to the American spirit of freedom. What a fine build-up he made for these ideas!

Dr. Van Kirk went one step farther. He mentioned "Bishop Francis J. McConnell of the Methodist Church" and others as being "prophets of a new social order," who, in advocating these social ideas, "were charged with being radicals, socialists, and what have you." Bishop McConnell and those who drafted the Social Ideals were radicals and still are—not because they favored collective bargaining, but because they rejected the profit motive. It is indeed interesting to see Dr. Van Kirk use his free radio time to try to take some of the sting out of these charges and further influence the people in behalf of this radicalism.

The Philadelphia *Inquirer* for April 29, 1945, carried a story that illustrates the way in which the Federal Council is promoting its communistic ideas through the co-operatives. It gives us the popular appeal and would naturally lead people to think that the co-operative movement was a real Christian enterprise. The Federal Council's name is mentioned, monopolies are condemned, and it is stated that people save money under the new system. It is interesting for the sake of our book to observe that the very men whom we have mentioned are here active. The story in full follows:

"PARLEY URGES EXTENSION OF CO-OP MOVEMENT HERE

"Extension of the principle of sales and production co-operatives, was advocated yesterday by speakers at a regional conference on church, labor and consumer co-operation, sponsored by the Federal Council of Churches of Christ in America.

"The conference was held in the Broadwood Hotel and was indorsed by the Central Labor Union (A.F.L.), the Philadelphia Industrial Union Council (C.I.O.), and the Philadelphia Area Co-operative Federation.

"Voorhis Raps Monopolies

"Representative Jerry Voorhis, of California, the principal speaker, said that 'unemployment is the greatest of domestic problems, and is largely caused by monopolies on economies, which tend for low production and high prices.'

"He described co-operatives as a 'non-Governmental way for breaking monopolies' and asserted that co-operatives have the effect of increasing the purchasing power of consumers' dollar by 15 per cent.

"Expansion Is Urged

"Clinton S. Golden, assistant to the president of the

United Steel Workers and a vice chairman of the War Production Board, said that up to the present time participation in co-operatives has frequently been confined to union members and urged that in the future they should expand their scope beyond union members and enter 'the larger open market.'

"Another speaker was Rev. Nelson H. Cruikshank, director of social insurance activities of the A.F.L. Dr. J. Henry Carpenter presided, and a panel discussion was led by Dr. Benson Y. Landis, of the Federal Council of Churches."

New York State recently had a big battle over what is called the Ives-Quinn Bill. The Federal Council threw its entire weight in behalf of the passing of the bill. This bill makes it unlawful for a man to consider the religious belief or color of any person whom he employs, and any such discrimination on the part of the employer may cost him, not only a heavy fine, but also a term in jail. There are many businesses where what a man believes determines his usefulness to that business. The Federal Council again threw its weight on the side of collectivism in this fight. New York State is the first state in the union to adopt such legislation, but it is the opening wedge for similar legislation in every state in the union.

One very interesting angle to this picture we should not overlook. *Our Sunday Visitor* for April 29, 1945, a powerful Roman Catholic weekly published in the United States, speaks of *The Protestant,* a magazine published in New York, as "a New York pro-Communist magazine." In the same article, referring to the resolution adopted by the Inter-American Labor Congress, we read: "A resolution adopted at that Convention furnished the clue to the interpretation of Communist-Protestant cooperation in many parts of the United States." Why does the Roman Catholic organ speak of the Communist-Protestant, and why does it call *The Protestant* a "pro-Communist magazine"? The answer is that *Our Sunday Visitor* is not asleep. It has its eyes open to the Federal Council propaganda. One of the leaders of the Federal Council movement is the editor of *The Protestant*. Furthermore, the communistic elements in the United States are aware of the fact that their closest companions, blood brothers, are none other than the leaders in the Federal Council of the Churches of Christ in America. The Roman Catholic element—with the exception of a small group which has been vigorously propagating the Federal Council's idea—actually puts the two words together—"Communist-Protestant cooperation in many parts of the United States." Of course, from our position, these communists who are actually in the churches are not Protestants at all. Anything truly Protestant stands by the Protestant creeds!

These are strong forces that are operating in the United States—these communistic elements and these church elements; and with the strength and encouragement that they have received from the turn in world events and Russia's coming to a place of power, the ardor of these groups is not going to diminish. They have been encouraged, as Earl Browder declares, and in the post-war world America is going to hear from them as it has never heard before. In the labor movements, in the educational world, in places of government, and above all within the church of Jesus Christ, or what is called the church of Jesus Christ, these communistic ideas, the germ idea of collectivism is entrenched and will exercise power it has never had before in the history of the land. These forces are going to combine and unite as never before.

America, the road ahead is perilous. The forces in this battle are strong; they are organized. Their recruits are young and aggressive, and their number is on the increase.

Let us now consider what real, constructive efforts should be made to wage this battle. First, it must be said: Only from the position and vantage point of the Bible and the historic Christian faith can any stand be made and any battle waged. Men must come all the way back to this position and not attempt to stop at some half-way or compromising point. For instance, present-day Barthianism is not the historic position of the church, and to stop there is to take refuge in a "new modernism." The ablest spokesman of this falsehood in America today is Reinhold Niebuhr of Union Theological Seminary, New York.

The ground lost must be regained. The finest illustration of this was the conquest and fall of Germany. She drove to Stalingrad; but the ground was retaken in the drive back to Berlin. She conquered Europe and moved into Egypt; we drove her back across North Africa, Sicily, Italy, France, and into Germany, and to surrender. All the ground lost in maintaining our American ideals and concept of freedom must be regained. This indicates the magnitude of the task before us.

The most important and by far the most valuable thing that has been done up to the present time has been the formation in 1941 of the American Council of Christian Churches. Until that time the Federal Council had been alone and undisputed in its field, and its claim to speak for Protestantism was unchallenged. The American Council, now consisting of fourteen Protestant denominations which have banded together as a council of churches to challenge the right of the Federal Council to be the voice of Protestantism, to expose its near-communism and its radicalism, and to lift a banner in behalf of the historic Christian faith, has done more than any other one thing to shake the religious forces of the country and to raise these vital questions in church after church, congregation after congregation, and in the mind of individual after individual.

The full story of the development and the advance of the American Council has been given in our recent volume, "Twentieth Century Reformation." This Council is accomplishing its purpose far more quickly than any of those who had a part in its establishment ever dreamed. It is the spearhead of the reformation movement in Protestantism, and thousands have turned to it with real hope and enthusiasm. This Council adopted a doctrinal platform setting forth the historic truths of the Protestant faith, the common denominator which all Protestant denominations historically have held.

The American Council has called and is calling people out of the Federal Council. It has clearly and fearlessly announced and proclaimed that it is the duty of the Lord's people, in the light of the Scriptures, to have nothing to do with the Federal Council; to repudiate it, to withdraw from it, to expose it, to warn people everywhere of its false message and the peril of its leadership.

The American Council, during its spring meeting, May 2-4, Grand Rapids, Michigan, sent the following message to the United States delegation at the San Francisco conference:

"ON LIBERTY, JUSTICE, AND PEACE

"To the American Delegation at the San Francisco Conference:

"The American Council of Christian Churches, assembled in session at Grand Rapids, Michigan, assures you of our earnest prayers. We have prayed for you, our American delegation, and for the whole conference. We are deeply concerned lest America and the world place their hopes in any plans for peace that may be unsound and illusory. We fear that the present emphasis upon the establishment of permanent peace at any price will jeopardize the principles of justice and liberty for all. We shall lose the peace if we compromise in international relationships with any concept of freedom which is below that upon which our own country is based. To do so means that our American concept of freedom must be sacrificed. It is for that American concept of freedom, and no other, that our sons and daughters are laying down their lives.

"We are well aware that the Federal Council of Churches and other leftist and pacifist organizations are attending the conference in an effort to influence its decisions. In this leftist attitude, which has a different concept of freedom, the Federal Council does not represent the thought of most Protestants. It would be better for the civilized world not to have a peace organization than to have one committed to the continual appeasement of forces inimical to the Christian, American concept of freedom.

"Almighty God, who has given us the freedom we now enjoy, will continue this blessing to us only as we maintain it in deed as well as in word. 'Blessed is the nation whose God is the Lord.'

"(A copy of this message is being sent to President Truman.)"

There can be no compromise with communism. Every time compromise is made with the ideology of communism, liberty is sacrificed and lost. It is in the light of this truth that the clear, clean-cut testimony of the American Council—its uncompromising position in regard to unbelief and to the Federal Council's social order—has commended the Council and has given it such a testimony and opportunity for service in the saving of our American way of life, at the same time bearing testimony to the great truths of the Christian faith.

It is only natural that in such a battle there would be many who would like to compromise. The world is always full of compromisers. Compromise is the most popular word that Satan ever coined. When principle is involved and liberty is at stake, truth can never be compromised with error.

Since the American Council came into existence in 1941 another group, built upon the principle of compromise,—not attacking or exposing the Federal Council, but working silently along with it,—has come into existence. We mention it here simply to answer questions that people might have about it. It is the National Association of Evangelicals whose leader is Mr. J. Elwin Wright. Nearly all of its leaders are men who are members of the Federal Council and a part of the Federal Council's program. They are not willing to take any stand that will in any way jeopardize their position or security inside the Federal Council fold. They are, in the terms of modern battle, the collaborators, the Petains and Lavals, in contrast to the De Gaulles and Churchills. There has never been an issue at any stage in the history of the world where there were not always some who took such a position. This group serves a good and healthy purpose so far as clarifying the atmosphere is concerned.

There is the Federal Council with its radical program;

there is the American Council with its clear-cut, uncompromising loyalty to the Word of God; there is the N.A.E. with its middle-of-the-road, appeasement attitude. This may confuse some for a little while, but it only strengthens and clarifies the issues for men everywhere, just as the stand of De Gaulle and Churchill has done for the whole world. Laval and Petain have finally had to come back to France to face retributive justice. It always works that way.

Every churchman in the United States, every man who is a member of a church in the land of America, has to face these issues. If his denomination is in the Federal Council, it should be gotten out, and if it cannot be gotten out, the local church to which that man belongs should withdraw from the denomination; if the local church cannot withdraw, the man and his family should withdraw. We must have true churches, not near-communistic churches, not churches as units of the revolution. We must have churches that take the historic terms of the faith and use them in their historic meaning. The Federal Council is doing in the economic and political world exactly what it has done in the religious world. It has stolen the terminology of democracy to use in behalf of a false social notion. Men everywhere must be put on their guard as to this condition and be willing to make any and every sacrifice possible to preserve freedom.

The church of the Lord Jesus Christ is a glorious and powerful institution. He gave it to the world and promised to bless it. He alone is its Head and King. It is truly this glorious church, terrible as an army with banners, that America needs in this hour and that the Lord's people everywhere must help to build. They must build it not only for themselves, but also for their children; build it not only for the blessing of the land, but also for the glory of God. The whole armor of God must be put on. Prayer is a constant help and vital weapon. Truly this is the battle for the Christian.

Even at this present time the Federal Council leaders have so embraced the idea of controlling and directing the affairs of society that they have endeavored actually to control the time given free on the great networks to religion. They have used and are using their influence to keep any of this free time from going into the hands of the American Council, the Federal Council's one adversary. When the American Council spoke up and asked for its share of the free time given to Protestants, leaders in the Federal Council bitterly and vigorously opposed the American Council's being given a moment of time.

Dr. J. Henry Carpenter, of whom we have had considerable to say in this discussion, wrote a long letter to the president of the Blue Network of the American Broadcasting System, protesting the granting of radio time to the American Council, which he described as "one of those disruptive, negative forces which often times develops in a community, or even in a nation, and which has been built up because certain people could not get their own way. . . . Any thinking man will realize that this is exactly the opposite of what we must build if we are going to have a nation and a world of strength and of peace." (From *The Witness* for March 23, 1944, published by the Episcopal Church Publishing Co.)

The position here taken boldly is that we can have world peace by keeping the Gospel away from the people. This fits Dr. Carpenter's book perfectly. We can have peace only in the collectivistic co-operative, and this is established by first destroying our free economy which the Gospel gave us. So we must keep the Gospel that demands a free economy away from the people!

If Dr. Carpenter and his colleagues, in an attempt to control radio and keep from the people the message of the historic Christian faith, are willing to go this far in a free America, how far will they go when they actually control society itself? Will it be the firing squad?

All this belies the bland, sweet words of tolerance, respect for minority rights, and liberty for all, which many of these Federal Council men so smilingly use.

The leaders of the Federal Council are also behind the movement in the United States to have radio stations refuse to sell time to religion. It is the evangelicals, who believe in the historic Christian faith, who buy the time on the air and preach the Gospel. The Federal Council groups are not able to buy the time, or, at least, to sustain their programs by the free will gifts of the people. The people are not interested in their kind of talk. So the Federal Council leaders have launched the attack that is being made upon the Gospel programs.

It was the Federal Council spokesmen in Philadelphia who were behind the move that resulted in Station WPEN, on April 2, 1945, cancelling all of its paid religious contracts, arbitrarily cutting off sixteen Gospel programs, and announcing that it was going to give time free. All the free Protestant time on this station has gone into the hands of the Federal Council men.

A tremendous protest was made to this move of Station WPEN. A mammoth rally was held in Convention Hall, Philadelphia, attended by 14,500 people, as a result of this action. The broadcast that we had had for more than ten years they arbitrarily cut off, and this particular study, "Private Enterprise in the Scriptures," turned out to be our last broadcast series. The station has now given the hour which we previously bought in the open market to the Federal Council group who control the local church federation.

One of the leaders of this federation is the Rev. George Emerson Barnes, outstanding modernist and a representative of the Presbyterian Church, U.S.A., in the Federal Council, and a confidant of its inner circle. He led the fight to put the federation on record approving WPEN's policy to "control religion" and remove it from the "free market" where time could be bought by Gospel-loving people and churches to preach the Gospel.

Religion has as much right to buy time on the radio as any group in our free America. In thus attempting to remove religion from the free market, radio is being left more completely in the hands of secularism.

It stands to reason, moreover, that if the social program which the Federal Council advocates is ever to be adopted in the United States, the clear-cut presentation of the Gospel of Jesus Christ, which gave us our free economy and liberty, must be watered down or kept entirely from the people. If they can succeed in keeping the real Gospel from reaching the people, and, instead, present another gospel in the terms of the historic Christian faith, as they are endeavoring to do, they will be able to lead America into a controlled economy. It is this type of control that every American must vigorously resist.

What has happened in Philadelphia is happening in city after city where Federal Council leaders and representatives, working in the closest co-operation with Federal Council headquarters, are maneuvering to have the Gospel put off the air, and in the name of tolerance and fair play monopolize the religion that the radio audience shall receive.

This battle, however, continues outside the church in the educational world, the political world, the medical world. The totalitarianism of the ideas offered by the Federal Council covers the whole sphere of life, and men in every branch, every activity, every endeavor are involved, and crumpled together in one mass by the grasp of the tyrant's hand.

Socialized medicine is nothing more than the totalitarian principle at work in the medical world. Every liberty-loving American should oppose it and demand free medicine. Every issue that we have discussed between a controlled economy and private enterprise is involved between socialized medicine and free medicine. The businessman, the laboring man, the baker, the plumber, the druggist, the butcher, the barber, the lawyer, the undertaker—all—are involved. The Congress of the United States and the assembly of every state are involved.

It is in the legislative chambers of Congress that these issues come to battle. Social advances that can be made within the structure of free society should be made. Social advances that are not advances, but transgressions of the principles of freedom, and which involve the idea of collectivism, should be resisted. Congressmen must put freedom and principle above votes, and, if necessary, sacrifice their office rather than compromise with the principles of freedom. We need men in office who will stand for freedom, not just talk about it! Liberty is not always lost in one great battle. It is inch by inch, little by little, step by step, that liberty is whittled away. The pattern of the enemy's attack is usually the same. He comes with his social program, announcing that it is in keeping with the American way of life, that there is nothing wrong with it; and then he gets the gain; but there has been a transgression upon the principle of freedom. Strengthened by that victory, he comes again and again and again, always in the name of the American idea of democracy.

Sooner or later, when people begin to awake to a realization of what has been happening, the enemy will change his line of defense and attack and announce that they have already embarked upon this program, that a number of the essential steps have already been taken, and that they must now logically go on or they will lose every gain they have made, or the previous gains will not be effective unless more total controls are imposed!

Perhaps the greatest thing, however, that can be done for the preservation of liberty is to present the great American ideals as they come from the Scriptures. All the instruments of propaganda in the nation should be used to that end. The educational system should wake up, turn from the road that leads to economic control, and return to the path of freedom. People must be educated, not lulled to sleep. It is a tremendous task, but it must be done, if America's freedom is to be saved. There must be a love for these issues, and that comes only with an understanding and a thorough appreciation of their significance and meaning.

Perhaps this explains more than any other one thing the conduct of the businessmen of the nation, as institution after institution has surrendered to the totalitarian conception of labor's "closed shop." Their idea has been to "let the other fellow do it; let him fight; we will make the best terms we can and go on." In such an idea America is lost. Why have men taken this attitude? It is not simply because they want to avoid a fight, but because they really do not believe strongly enough and with a sufficiently burning conviction to lead them to stand. They are not willing to sacrifice their businesses, if need be, for the principles of liberty on which they were established. It is more of the spirit of sacrifice for principle that we must have, or we are lost. If our boys could give their lives, surely we can fight in the post-war era to keep freedom.

We have called this volume, "The Rise of the Tyrant."
He will arise unless we individually, personally, in our several places, stand in his way. Wherever his ideas present
themselves we must refute them. We have endeavored to
point out the road on which the tyrant in America will ride.
The door is open, the gate is unlocked for his entrance and
appearance. We do not mean to say that the Federal Council
is this particular tyrant. Do not misunderstand us. So far as
this particular picture is concerned, the Federal Council is
the John the Baptist in the movement. It is announcing,
"Prepare ye the way, for the kingdom of God is at hand."

We have sought to show that it is not the kingdom of
God, but the kingdom of man or some other kingdom that
is being offered us. The Word of God supports freedom.
The modern church, having rejected the Word of God, offers
to us a system of tyranny while the historic Christian
church, remaining true to its creeds, lifts its voice in behalf
of freedom. It is in the train of such a tradition, it is in the
way of such a leadership, that we have sought to stand.

In standing in such a place we are assured of the favor of
God. After all, these problems and forces are beyond the
ken and power of men to understand and control. God
alone understands them. He alone has the power with which
to deal with them. That is why the Bible speaks out in
such resonant terms, "Righteousness exalteth a nation: but
sin is a reproach to any people" (Prov. 14:34), and "Blessed is
the nation whose God is the Lord" (Psa. 33:12). A nation
whose god is not the Lord, a nation whose god, such as in a
communistic state, is an anti-God, or whose god is the State,
cannot have the blessing and favor of the Almighty. He takes
liberty from them. But a nation that exalts and honors the
God of creation, the God of the Bible, the God and Father
of our Lord Jesus Christ, may have His blessing and favor. He

controls the minds of men, the fortunes of providence, and all the decisions of destiny. America early wrote upon her coins, "In God we trust," and if the trust of America will now be in God, in His truth, in the ideals of His Word, we shall have His favor and His deliverance.

Instead of turning to the Government to control the people, the forces of the church should turn to God in humiliation and confession of sin, and with a petition for a great revival. Lawlessness, immorality, drunkenness, dissipation, lying, stealing, murder, adultery, and the like, which abound and are on the increase, can be checked only through the preaching of the Gospel of the grace of God. America must come back to God or she shall go on to a near-communism. America must not listen to the voice of the modern church, or she shall go on to communism with its tyranny. She must come back at any cost to the sound of the voice of the true, historic church. The Sunday school must be rebuilt around the Bible. The church must be rebuilt around the cross of Christ, the blood that was shed for the ransom of the race. When we do this we are fighting the battle for freedom, and winning the battle for America. Everywhere must arise men who will declare, "I am not ashamed of the gospel of Christ: for it is the power of God unto salvation" (Rom. 1:16); "If the Son therefore shall make you free, ye shall be free indeed" (John 8:36). This is the liberty that America must have. Without it there are only tyranny, darkness, and death. Without it the road is paved with the smoothest possible macadam to speed the rise of the tyrant. The welfare of our children and the future of America depend upon the part we personally take in this battle for freedom. Let us arise! Let us march on!

ACKNOWLEDGMENTS

Quotations from the following publications have been used by permission of the publishers:

"The Road to Serfdom," by Friedrich A. Hayek; University of Chicago Press, Chicago, Ill.

"Peace through Co-operation," by J. Henry Carpenter; Harper & Brothers, New York, N. Y.

"Preaching in a Revolutionary Age," by G. Bromley Oxnam; Abingdon-Cokesbury Press, Nashville, Tenn.

"The Christ of the American Road," by E. Stanley Jones; Abingdon-Cokesbury Press, Nashville, Tenn.

"The Choice Before Us," by E. Stanley Jones; Abingdon-Cokesbury Press, Nashville, Tenn.

"The Soviet Spirit," by Harry F. Ward; International Publishers Co., Inc., New York, N. Y.

254

INDEX

255

INDEX OF SCRIPTURE